UMBRIA, THE MARCHES & SAN MARINO

Christopher Catling

PASSPORT BOOKS
a division of *NTC Publishing Group*
Lincolnwood, Illinois USA

rule is to avoid the coast, where industrialisation and tourism have done their worst. The only exception to be made is for Pesaro, where Giovanni Bellini's sublime *Coronation of the Virgin* in the Civic Museum stands forth as one of the greatest glories of Renaissance painting and whither the annual Musical Festival draws lovers of Rossini (who was born there) from all over the world. Otherwise, stay inland: and if you are looking for a still centre to which to return each evening – a much more satisfactory arrangement than a continuous tour, with its perpetual packing and unpacking, registering and paying of bills – choose somewhere in the neighbourhood of Urbino, which has always seemed to me more Umbrian than Marchesan (if that is the word) and must be one of the most rewarding cities for its size in all Italy.

As for San Marino, it should be said at once that its main interest is political rather than cultural. Like most other miniature nations of Europe such as Andorra, Monaco and Liechtenstein – but not like the Vatican City, which is obviously a separate phenomenon and a law unto itself – it has little to attract the visitor but its scenery, its climate and its own quaintness as a historical survival – the fact, in short, that it exists at all. Fortunately it needs no more than this to pull in the tourists in prodigious numbers, falling over each other to buy its stamps and its coins, and to photograph members of its exuberantly uniformed army – which, numbering as it does about a thousand, accounts for some ten per cent of the male population.

Rereading what I have written above, I greatly fear that I have exceeded my brief. My task was to introduce this book, rather than to supplement it with reflections of my own – reflections which are anyway of limited value since, with the important exception of Urbino (which I was able to visit only a month or two ago) it is now well over a decade since I have visited most of the places described in the pages that follow. The author of those pages, on the other hand, knows them as they are. He has criss-crossed the region not once but many times, and at every season of the year. And rightly – though he provides an answer for the vast majority of questions that the average educated traveller will wish to ask – he does not confine himself to matters art-historical. Most of us, after all, come to Italy on holiday; there is a limit to the amount of culture we can absorb, particularly on a hot summer day. How important it is, therefore, to know something about the local food and wine with which we are to reward ourselves when that day is done. (Or even, on occasion, rather earlier.) Here too, let Christopher Catling be your guide. You will not regret it.

1. INTRODUCTION

This guide covers the two central Italian provinces of Umbria and the Marches, along with the tiny Republic of San Marino. It is not intended to be comprehensive. The peace and beauty of the unspoiled hill towns that form the central theme of this book are in marked contrast to large areas of the Marches, which have been omitted because they are unrewarding for the traveller in search of a change from everyday pressures. The eastern half of the Marches has some undoubted attractions – the graceful loggias of the Piazza del Popolo in Ascoli Piceno, for example – but the whole of the Adriatic coast – from Pesaro to San Benedetto – is one continuous ribbon development, consisting of a narrow beach, backed by a railway and major road, lined by offices and factories and the numerous parallel valleys that debouch into the Adriatic are similarly developed.

Places which hold no great rewards have therefore been deliberately omitted from this guide, or given only passing mention, for I am of the belief that a good guide book should tell you about the best there is to see, rather than striving to be comprehensive.

It might be an idea to try struggling through the congested streets of Ascoli Piceno, just to discover how different, how delightful, by contrast, are the cities of Umbria and the mountainous regions of the Marches (they are called cities, even when they are little more than walled villages, just as they all have a 'cathedral' and every building of pretension is a *palazzo* – a palace).

But then, from whichever direction you approach the region, whether from the airports of Pisa, Rome or Bologna, you will already have seen enough of commercial and industrial Italy to appreciate that the very heart of Italy has, by happy circumstance, remained unspoilt; an area of small-scale agriculture, of steep-sided hills cut by deep ravines, of farmsteads, monasteries and ancient cities separated from the countryside only by vertiginous stone walls.

The region does not lack industry – principally around Terni, and in the drained lake bed that now forms the Vale of Spoleto – nor does one begrudge Umbrians the means of earning a livelihood, for the life goes out of a region if the young migrate elsewhere in search of material benefits, as they did from Umbria earlier this century; but you can also travel a whole day on minor roads, and see little that would startle any of the people who have lived, worked and died in the region at any time over the last three centuries.

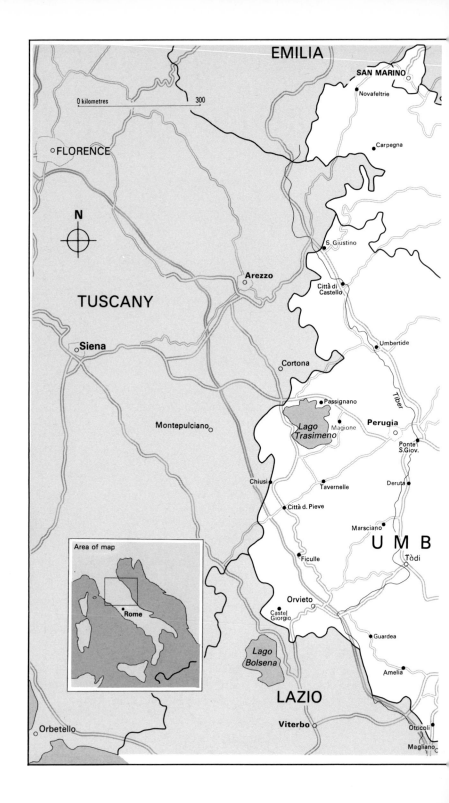

The dramatic Monti Sibillini range separates Umbria from the Marches

View over Lake Trasimeno

The hilltop towns of Umbria

Indeed, when you arrive at a little hilltop town, like Bettona, park the car and walk within the sheltering walls, there is a very real sense of stepping back several centuries and leaving the modern world behind.

In part this is because many towns now prohibit traffic from entering, or have streets so narrow that only the little three-wheeled motorised carts, scarcely more than a motorbike with a box on the back, can pass up and down them.

The exclusion of motorcars accounts for the unique sounds of a walled town. Early in the morning, or during the midday siesta, all is quiet except for the splash of the fountain, the clatter of a startled pigeon's wings as a cat steals by or the muffled sounds of meal preparation behind closed shutters.

In the afternoon, children come out to play, watched by their mothers who sit around the fountain with the older women of the town, knitting and swapping gossip. Old men silently play cards at folding tables outside cafes, blocking the pavement, and occasionally looking up to greet a passer by.

By early evening the square begins to fill with people, the younger ones now returned from work in nearby offices or factories. Strolling around the square, men arm in arm with men, women with women, everyone speaks in tones of intimacy, even when the subject is politics or business, and yet – in the absence of traffic – the sound of all this human conversation, echoing off the surrounding buildings, can rise to an extraordinary volume.

The passeggiata

The evening *passeggiata* is a custom not unique to Umbria and the Marches though here, perhaps, it has more significance. It helps to cement *campanalismo*, that bond of loyalty – some would say parochialism – that unites a community of people, all of whom were born within the sound of the town's ancient bells – a closeness and familiarity that cannot exist in a larger city.

Some say that the *passeggiata* is a warm-country phenomenon. Yet in the depths of frosty winter the same crowds throng the square; only then the men wear cashmere coats and silk scarves, if they can afford to, and the women furs, instead of summer's co-ordinated polo shirts and sneakers, leather belts and discrete jewellery. Looking good – *fare bella figura* – and establishing for all to see that one has made it in the world, is just one of the complex undertows running through the outwardly smooth current of the evening stroll, along with courtship, political lobbying and business wheeling and dealing.

Apart from the clothing, and the fact that unmarried girls are no longer chaperoned, the evening stroll is an aspect of town life that has changed little in centuries. It usually takes place in and around the main square – the Piazza del Popolo – against the backdrop of a group of equally ancient public buildings: the fountain, the town hall and the cathedral. These architectural monuments also form the main focus of interest for the traveller, privileged to share for a while the life and culture of a close-knit community.

The fountains

Most ancient will be the water source that feeds the fountain – the reason for the existence of a town here at all. Many fountains are ornate, the star of them all being Perugia's graceful Fontana Maggiore with its bas reliefs illustrating the Liberal Arts, Old Testament scenes, episodes from Aesop's fables and ancient Roman legend.

The decoration here and elsewhere indicates the importance of a reliable pure water supply to a people who were often at war with their neighbours and constantly under the threat of siege.

Most of these towns are built on hilltops at a height of 300m or more above sea-level. At this height water is scarce and any available springs, along with stormwater run-off, are channelled into reservoirs, with sufficient head of pressure to fill the fountains. Private water supplies were a luxury. Everyone collected their water from the communal supply (no doubt that explains why the fountain is still the focus of community gatherings) and laws protected the purity of the source, prohibiting 'beasts, barrels, unwashed pots and unclean hands' the use of the water.

Sunday morning in Bevagna

The cathedrals

Though many towns in Umbria and the Marches are ringed by pre-Roman walls and possess the remains of a Roman gate, a temple or a bathhouse, the oldest building still in use is likely to be the Duomo or cathedral. It may not play such an all-pervading role in Umbrian life as it did, but because of its former importance it too will be located in the main square.

To anyone used to the form and appearance of English or French Gothic churches, Italian cathedrals are plainly different. Façades can be grim – sometimes left unfinished as a craggy cliff of broken brick or stone. Light rarely floods the nave through great stained glass windows but steals in through portholes of muddy yellow glass.

Inside, the eye takes a while to adjust to the gloom and sometimes, then, the view is a great disappointment; for many a cathedral with a Romanesque exterior, promising considerable interest within, turns out to have a too-flamboyant, icing-sugar Baroque interior, the legacy of church refurbishment on a large scale in the 17th century.

Nevertheless, when you understand better the pattern of Italian church architecture you will experience the thrill that comes from discovering the exceptions; some small but telling departure from the norm, some rustic but unspoiled gem of the Romanesque period, or – better still – a church that declares its greater antiquity by the evident Roman influence.

For when Constantine the Great issued his Edict of Milan, in AD313, granting official status to the Christian religion, and once Christians began to emerge from their hidden inner rooms and catacomb chapels to worship openly and legally in public, they had to decide what type and style of building would be appropriate for the celebration of their liturgies, and they looked to existing public buildings as their model.

Some early Christians actually took over existing Roman temples. In Terni, the tiny church of San Salvatore has a circular sanctuary. Inside, the bare stone walls rise to form an elongated dome, shaped like a beehive. The dome is pierced by a round skylight, through which a shaft of sunlight penetrates at noon, focussing on the altar below – for this was originally a pagan temple dedicated to the worship of the sun.

Elsewhere church builders imitated classical temple architecture. At Clitunno, the 4th-century church of San Salvatore is raised on a stone plinth, fronted by a portico of Corinthian columns supporting a pediment. It might easily be mistaken for a temple to Clitunnus, the god of the nearby sacred springs, except for the Christian frescoes – and local people still call it the Tempietto, the little temple.

Other forms of architecture were also tried. In Perugia, the 5th-century church of Sant' Angelo is circular, a miniature Pantheon, while outside the city walls of Spoleto, the cemetery church of San Salvatore, built at the end of the 4th century, is a fascinating hybrid of reused domestic and temple masonry, salvaged from redundant Roman buildings nearby. This church, though, has a plan that approximates to the commonest type that you will see

The early Christian church known as the Tempietto del Clitunno was built in the style of a Roman Temple

all over the region – based on the Roman basilica, the hall of the magistrate and seat of local government. In its simplest form, the basilica consisted of a tall central nave, lit by a clerestory, flanked by lower, narrower side aisles. Internally, the nave and aisles were divided by columns, and the seat of the magistrate was raised on a dais at the far end, sometimes within a rectangular or semicircular apse.

Here and there, especially in the remoter parts of the Marches and Umbria, you will find churches built on precisely this model that have remained untouched by later improvers and restorers. In San Leo, near San Marino, or at Lugnano in Teverina, near Terni, you can walk into churches that differ from the Roman prototype only in that an altar now occupies the place of the magisterial chair, raised high above the nave with a crypt below sheltering the tomb of some local saint. The same sense of continuity between the Roman and Christian eras can be experienced in the early Romanesque churches of Sant' Eufemia and San Gregorio Maggiore in Spoleto, or the two small churches that face each other across the Piazza Silvestri in Bevagna, all of them enjoyable for their classical purity and simplicity.

In grander cathedrals the basilican plan is still detectable, but the aisles are here cluttered with side altars and the apse will have grown a cluster of chapels radiating from the eastern end. Some of them retain outstanding frescoes; notably the basilica in Assisi and the church at Montefalco, both dedicated to and celebrating the life and miracles of St Francis, or the apocalyptic frescoes of Luca Signorelli in the cathedral at Orvieto.

Too many of these grander churches have, however, suffered 'improvement' as a result of the counter-reformationary zeal of the 17th century or, as in the case of many churches in the Marches, necessitated by earthquake damage. Unless you have a taste for the gilded and painted stucco work and devotional paintings of the Baroque era, the interest of many large churches ceases at the façade.

One can only wonder why, at the same time as being grateful, so many of these ancient façades were not also demolished and rebuilt. They can hardly have appealed to 17th-century taste or notions of propriety since the masons and sculptors of the Romanesque age never limited their scope to the carving of purely religious subjects. We find birds and beasts half remembered from some distant Roman art, or copied from late Roman sarcophagi, celebrations of rural pursuits, the grape harvest, drunkenness, brawling and furtive love-making. Lion-like beasts guard the church portals, gnawing on the head of a human or eating their own offspring. Doors are often framed by friezes of acanthus, vineleaf and lily flowers, inhabited by real and mythical beasts, including penguins and crocodiles at Assisi. Caryatids strain comically to uphold the fabric of the façade and devils and angels fight over the soul of a dying man. Then, above the portals, the gable is pierced by the beautiful rose or wheel window that all the great 11th- to 13th-century churches of the region possess; concentric circles infilled with complex geometric loops and mouchettes, some decorated with cosmati work and many as delicate as lace.

These are the shapes and patterns that will draw your eye across many a main square in the region, inviting you to come closer; endlessly rewarding for anyone with the foresight to bring binoculars and the patience to study the details.

The town halls

Nearby, often alongside the church or opposite, you will then discov\
more austere façade of the town hall, partnered by its campanile. Ma\
these town halls date from the 15th century, although some were begun
earlier, their construction interrupted by civil strife or the ravages of the Black
Death which raged through Europe from 1340 to 1430 and carried off more
than half the population of numerous Italian towns. Called *palazzi* (palaces)
they represented an ideal rarely achieved at the time of their construction:
the ideal of local, democratic government by representatives of the merchant
guilds, the aristocracy and the people. Representatives (*priori*) were elected,
in theory, to serve for a finite time (sometimes as little as two months) so that
no one individual could dominate local government. In practice, instead of
broadly based government, wealthy *signori* (aristocrats) were able to impose
their own personal authority and, in some instances, establish virtual heredi-
tary dynasties.

Even so, the town hall, built at public expense via a system of taxes and
rates, provided the focus for local decision-making and the administration of
justice. Councillors, officials and leading citizens met to debate in the Great
Hall. Official pronouncements were made to the public from a balcony or
raised platform, called the *ringheria*, in front of the building; the term gave
rise to the verb 'to harangue', which perhaps indicates the nature in which
proclamations were given and received. Criminals were tried in the Great
Hall and guilty ones often exposed to the searing sun and the insults of the
crowd in a cage in front of the hall; such a cage of iron still survives projecting
from a buttress on the corner of Gubbio's town hall. The bells of the tall
campanile alongside the hall would be used to warn citizens of impending
peril, to signal a military victory or to gather the people to an assembly.

Such grave and weighty matters as war and justice seem to have demanded
a suitably austere architectural style, for many town halls are grim, ponderous,
four-square buildings, battlemented and lacking exterior adornment. Decoration, where it exists – in Perugia or Gubbio for example – consists of a flight
of stone stairs or stone *stele*, the coats of arms of leading guilds and aristocrats
applied to the façade.

The interiors, though, could often be splendid, with magnificent painted
and gilded wooden ceilings or, as at Perugia, gorgeously coloured frescoes.
Now that so many town halls also serve as the *pinocoteca* or *museo civico* –
the art gallery or municipal museum – there is every opportunity to visit them
and admire their Renaissance splendour.

The castles

Fountain, cathedral, town hall – these three alone make a visit to almost any
hilltop town in the region a rewarding exploration. In addition, many have a
rocca or *fortezza* (castle or fortress), usually integral with the town's defensive
walls and occupying the highest point on the hill. Even where they are now

in ruins, or have lost their 12th- and 13th-century appearance because of remodelling in the Napoleonic era, their cliffside or hilltop locations make them worth visiting for the views alone.

The most intriguing of these castles, some dating to the period when the Lombards were in control of central Italy, line the narrow Valnerina, the wild valley of the River Nera that links Umbria to the Marches. Here the little-visited settlements, clinging to the mountainsides, are almost more fortress than village. You will need to be as agile as the mountain goats who graze the nearby slopes to explore fully the outlying walls and towers of these fortifications; some with lengths of wall winding down from hilltop to valley floor, like a miniature Great Wall of China, effectively funnelling all travellers through a narrow pass where the legitimacy of their business could be checked, or a small bribe extracted before onward passage was permitted.

There are, though, many more accessible castles: in San Marino, where the Cesta, or Fratta, fortress – now a museum of ancient armour – crowns the peak of Mount Titano, with a sheer drop below to wild wooded gorges; in nearby San Leo where the majestic Forte, with its cylindrical towers growing straight out of the rocky hilltop, was much admired by Macchiavelli, who described it as the finest military stronghold in Italy; and at Spoleto, where the magnificent Renaissance Rocca, once the centre of papal power in the region and – until recently – a maximum security prison, is being restored to its former splendour and will soon reopen as a museum and cultural centre.

So often these castles occupy the highest point in the city or town, as if deliberately positioned to provide a focal point in the landscape. The reasons were as much strategic as aesthetic: for the castles were intended to be highly visible to any would-be attacker. Approaching from the plain, bands of mercenaries, like the notorious 'White Company' of Sir John Hawkwood, would see an apparently impregnable city, enclosed within high walls and dominated by its fortress. That is the same view that the traveller sees today, and it is a view that now arrests us by its beauty rather than as an expression of strength. White walls, as often as not built by the pre-Roman Umbrian or Etruscan founders of the city, encircle tier upon tier of white and pink-walled houses, rising on stepped terraces to the tip of the hill, where a castle, or sometimes a cathedral dome, stands proud against the blue sky.

These cone-shaped cities, built out of the abundant local limestone, seem to look as fresh in the sunlight, contrasted against the deep green of the surrounding mountains, as they did when they were newly built in the 13th, 14th and 15th centuries.

Streets and homes

The sun beats down on these towns, but within the walls, the tall buildings, separated by the narrowest of streets and alleyways, cast a welcome deep shade. The whole city seems to be of stone – the streets and squares are paved and cobbled with it, and the steeper alleyways are made like stone staircases, with steps hollowed by centuries of pedestrian traffic. The houses may seem grim: their flat façades, pierced by simple rectangles for doors and windows, have little adornment – although in Assisi and Gubbio especially you will often see doorways with attractive 'depressed' arches, the haunches thickening as they rise, and with a teardrop-shaped keystone at the crown.

These houses, with their iron window grilles and battered, time-worn wooden doors, may look abandoned and uninhabited, at least at street level. Then, a door opens, a child slips out on the way to school, and you catch a glimpse within of a marbled or tiled staircase, leading steeply upwards – for, in these hilltop cities, people still live on the first floor, the *piano nobile*, rarely on the ground. The ground floor is used for storage instead, and once, in more dangerous times, could be used to delay your enemies, by dropping missiles through the floorboards on to the heads of any invader below.

Some ground floors have been converted to shops, or are used as workshops, where you will see coffin-makers, printers, bakers or motor mechanics at work as you wander the back alleys.

Most, though, are stacked with neat piles of wood, fuel for the winter and for the oven – for grandmother often still cooks pizza in a traditional wood-fired oven, even if her daughters have the latest kitchen technology. By the piles of wood you will also see great dusty carboys of green glass, used for storing wine, or smaller jars of vinegar or precious green olive oil. These products of the countryside, bought from local producers, represent the link which the town dwellers have with their country neighbours. Once the farmers themselves lived within the town walls for safety, but the countryside of Umbria and the Marches is now filled with farmhouses, built from the 17th century and onwards, when the fear of raids and pillage was over.

The landscape

Farming

Farming in the region is still a small-scale activity – by necessity, since the fields won from the hillsides are small and steep. The beautiful deer-like white cattle of Umbria, once used for ploughing, are now a rare sight, and small Fiat tractors, powerful enough to cope with steep inclines, have taken over their role. Even so, you will see no prairie farms or agro-industry here. The farming is, as often as not, organic – the fields manured with animal waste, the weeding done by hoe – simply because the farmers cannot afford the chemicals. The products of their labours – grapes, artichokes, wine and olives, milk and cheese, pork and chickens fed on home-grown maize – are sold in local markets or to local shopkeepers, not into some vast co-operative. Some farmers produce just enough from their yearly toil to feed themselves and make enough cash to keep themselves in clothes, petrol and other necessities. Ruined farmhouses, abandoned by owners who could not make ends meet, or whose sons were unwilling to inherit a life of back-breaking toil, are a common sight.

Though increasingly rare, it is still possible to see Umbrian white cattle, originally bred for sacrifice by the ancient Romans

Some farmers, though, are beginning to diversify; the flatter fields, down towards the plains of Umbria, are a blaze of yellow-headed sunflowers in June, while other fields are heady with the fragrance of tobacco flowers. As elsewhere in Europe, polythene tunnels are becoming a feature of the landscape, sheltering tomato, pepper and melon crops which, if produced early enough in the year, command a valuable price premium.

Another familiar sight is the green 'Agriturismo' sign, indicating a farm that offers bed, evening meal and breakfast to visiting tourists. Best of all, bringing a windfall to the owners of tumbledown farmhouses, the market for rural property is now lively, as foreigners seek an idyllic retreat in a region that is greener, less developed and cheaper than neighbouring Tuscany – and yet only an hour or so's drive from the international airports at Rome and Pisa.

These changes largely benefit the farmers who live in the foothills and plains of central Umbria. Heading eastwards, up and into the Apennines, which form the border and watershed between the Marches and Umbria, cultivated fields become much scarcer, and instead the rural population lives from rearing pigs for ham and sausages, and sheep for wool, meat and cheese. You will more rarely see the small pigs that produce the sweet prosciutto, for which the Marches is famed – since these are often reared in the shade, indoors.

You may, though, when passing through remote mountain hamlets, be barked at and chased by fierce white-haired sheepdogs, regarding your car as an unwanted, perhaps dangerous, intruder.

When you stop for a picnic in the high mountains, above the ever-consistent buzz of insects, you will always hear the distant sound of sheep-bells, and sometimes you will catch sight of a shepherd sitting in the shade of a rock or tree.

Flora and fauna

You will also, depending on the time of year, be astounded by the colour and profusion of the wild flowers. The same limestone that makes the region's hilltop towns gleam bright in the sunshine, and that, weathered by ice and snow and cut by fast-flowing meltwaters, makes the landscape so dramatic, also provides the conditions that bulbs, alpines and myriad lime-loving plants need in order to thrive. Even in winter, roadside verges support wild hellebores and spurges with their vivid lime-green flowers, and in spring to early summer the countryside around Assisi is famed for its glorious display of irises. In summer, any scrap of uncultivated land will be a patchwork of sky-blue chicory, small pink convolvulus, wild perennial sweet peas, white campion and ox-eye daisy, cut-leaved geraniums and the ubiquitous pink and red-flowered mallows – while shady walls and damp rock faces will be covered in small ferns and yellow and white-flowered saxifrages.

These flowers, and the butterflies that feed on them, delight the eye even if you are not a passionate plant lover, but for the real connoisseur, the highlight of a visit to the region must be the slopes of Monte Sibillini, north of Norcia, around the hamlets of Castelluccio and San Lorenzo, noted for rare and abundant Alpine flora as well as an exhilarating landscape.

Other forms of wildlife flourish in the dense acacia, chestnut and holm oak woodlands that carpet the hills of the region's officially protected Parco Naturale – east of Assisi, and west of Sassoferrato: red squirrels, wild boar and porcupines all flourish here, while the marshy shores of Lakes Trasimeno and Piediluco are populated by waders, herons and wildfowl.

For this reason, the sobriquet that has long been attached to the name of Umbria – Green Heart of Italy – now has a new, contemporary relevance. It was entirely appropriate that the World Wide Fund for Nature should have held a major conference in 1988 in Assisi – even more apt that Umbria's best-known local saint, Francis of Assisi, should have been proclaimed patron saint of ecology in 1979. Nor, growing up in such a beautiful region, would St Francis himself have failed to fall in love with the sun, moon, stars, birds, fruits and flowers of God's Creation – though to celebrate nature was a distinctly odd thing to do in the 13th century.

Happily, the charms of St Francis's environment, the hilltowns and churches, the wooded valleys and the high mountains, the wildlife and the dramatic scenery, are not those which appeal to tourists en masse – yet they are, for those who prefer quiet pleasures, the stuff of which memorable holidays are made.

2. HISTORY

The Etruscans and the Umbrians

The River Tevere (Tiber) once marked the boundary between the territories of the Etruscans and the Umbrians. These two ancient peoples were the first to leave any mark on central Italy. Of the **Etruscans** little is known and of the Umbrians even less. Their presence in Italy has been dated by archaeologists to the beginning of the 8th century BC but whether they were indigenous people or invaders from elsewhere remains a mystery. The strange Etruscan language, which has affinities with Sanskrit, has led some scholars to argue, controversially, that they came from the distant east, while others suggest they invaded from nearer shores: from Anatolia or Greece. On the other hand, the Etruscans regarded themselves as natives, and recent archaeological excavation seems to confirm this; their language and culture may have developed through trade contacts with the Phoenicians and Greeks.

The Etruscan remains in Perugia's Museo Archaeologica Nazionale dell' Umbria show ample evidence for such trading links. The Etruscans were skilled bronze casters and traded their weapons and armour for luxury goods, including ceramics: the museum is full of black and red figure vases, decorated with scenes from Greek mythology, and of accomplished Etruscan bronzework – mirrors, jewellery, armour and votive statues.

This rich array of material, excavated from tombs in and around Perugia, is an indication of the city's former importance. Along with Orvieto, it was one of the 12 great Etruscan cities that formed a loose political confederation, called the Dodecapolis; even today, Orvieto seems more like a Tuscan city, with its Sienese-inspired architecture, and Perugians speak Italian with a different harsher accent to that of the rest of Umbria.

Of the **Umbrians** themselves, scarcely anything remains; just some monolithic walls, underpinning the later Roman and medieval defences, that surround the hilltop towns they founded; the Eugubine Tablets in Gubbio, recording some of their religious practices, and a circular church in Terni which might have been a temple to the sun.

Both tribes worshipped a complex pantheon of naturalistic deities and their priests were renowned for their skills in augury: reading the will of the gods in natural phenomena, such as the pattern of birds in flight, in forks of lightning or in the organs of sacrificial animals. They cannot have foreseen, however, that the small trading post they established in the late 8th century BC, later to be called Rome, would one day eclipse their own culture.

The Romans

The Romans seem to have conquered their neighbours with relative ease. Perugia was defeated in 309BC and the other members of the Etruscan alliance were not long in acknowledging the power of Rome. Perhaps this was partly due to the subtlety of Roman strategy. Rather than occupy the hilltop cities of the Etruscans and Umbrians, the Romans created new towns in the plains; these coloniae, retirement settlements for army veterans, were strung out along the strategic Via Flaminia, the road built to provide a swift route between Rome and the northern frontiers of the expanding republic.

Gradually the prosperity of these towns eclipsed that of the ancient hilltop cities and little by little the Umbrians and Etruscans, still nominally indepen-dent allies of the Romans, were integrated into the new regime. The Romans, in turn, absorbed something of the Etruscans' religious beliefs; Roman legions all employed Etruscan augurers to propitiate the gods before an important battle, and the sacred white bulls of Umbria were the essential accompaniment to the triumphal processions of military heroes and emperors.

The Battle of Lake Trasimeno

The augurs were much in demand during the spring of 217BC, when – as Livy tells us in his history of Rome – many strange events occurred. The previous year the 30-year-old Carthaginian army general, **Hannibal**, appeared over the Alps, complete with Numidian cavalry, Gallic bowmen, Spanish infantry and elephants. After a difficult winter, Hannibal set out to cross the Apennines and see if he could persuade the Etruscans to abandon their Roman allies, as the Gauls had already done, and join with him in the final onslaught on Rome itself.

Meanwhile, in Rome, the statue of Mars on the Appian Way broke into a sweat, soldiers' spears burst spontaneously into flames and two moons rose in the sky. Major sacrifices were ordered to Jupiter, Juno and Minerva, but all to no avail. The famous battle of Lake Trasimeno was to result in the greatest defeat the Roman army suffered in its entire history.

Lake Trasimeno today is Umbria's summer playground. Ringed by holiday resorts, camp sites, watersports centres and even funfairs, it has long lost the unspoiled charm it once had when small fishing communities lived by catching eel, pike and perch along the reed-fringed shores.

Yet amidst the resorts there is an ominous spot on the map just north of the lake, and almost on the border with Tuscany, marked with a pair of crossed swords and called Sanguineto. If you seek it out, you will drive up a farm track to a natural amphitheatre, closed on three sides by hills and open to the south and the shores of Lake Trasimeno.

With Livy in hand, you can retrace the events of the battle, for the topography is exactly as Livy described. Hannibal, arriving here first, hid the majority of his troops in the surrounding hills and left a small contingent camped in the plain. The Romans arrived in the early morning, while the mist was still thick, and watched the rump of the Carthaginian army decamp and begin to march northwards, up into the hills. The Roman commander, **Flaminius**, assumed that the Carthaginians were fleeing, and happily brought his troops in after them.

Suddenly Hannibal's troops poured out of the hills, surrounding the Romans on all sides, and they, unprepared for the attack, had no time to organise themselves into fighting formation. In the chaos and panic that ensued, it was every man for himself, and, as Livy tells us, 'so great was the fury of the struggle, so totally absorbed was every man in its grim immediacy, that no one even noticed the earthquake which ruined large parts of many Italian towns, altered the course of swift rivers, brought the sea flooding into estuaries and started avalanches in the mountains.'

To this Wagnerian accompaniment, the Romans were massacred; many drowned in the lake as they stumbled over each other in the panic to escape; 15,000 died and only 10,000 survived. Hannibal marched on to harry the Romans for many more years, though never again to achieve such an important victory so close to Rome itself.

Hannibal had counted on the people of Umbria joining him on his onslaught on Rome, but they, on the contrary, remained loyal to their Roman allies. Spoleto sent Hannibal packing – an event commemorated by the city's Porta Fuga, the Gate of Flight.

The siege of Perugia

Umbria does not feature again in ancient history until the 1st century BC. An Etruscan soothsayer warned Caesar to beware the Ides of March. He was stabbed to death in the Senate on 15 March 44BC. In the aftermath of his murder, three rivals emerged for the title of emperor; Caesar's great-nephew, Octavius, Mark Antony and his brother Lucius. **Lucius** chose to make Perugia his base, and **Octavius** lay siege to the city in 40BC.

After seven months the starving Perugians finally caved in; ashamed at the ignominy of their defeat, one leading Perugian decided to commit suicide by setting fire to his home, and before long the whole city was ablaze. Spared the necessity of destroying the town, Octavius declared himself the Emperor Augustus, and out of the ashes of Perugia thus came the dawn of the new Imperial Age, the age of the Pax Romana when, for some 200 years, Italy enjoyed a period of unity and peace never to be seen again until the modern era.

The lasting legacy of the Romans in Umbria and the Marches is the **Via Flaminia**. This major artery, completed in 222BC, brought prosperity to the region. It was the route by which the new religion of Christianity was introduced to the region by Syrian merchants who, landing at Ancona or Ostia (the port of Rome), travelled up and down the highway, buying and selling and spreading the Gospel message. It was also to provide a swift and effective route along which barbarian invaders from the north swept into the heart of Italy towards the end of the 4th century.

The North–South Divide

The events that occurred in Umbria and the Marches at this time were to set the pattern for the next nine centuries. It is essentially a story of territorial conflict between northerners from beyond the Alps and southerners, in the form of the Church based in Rome, a Church which was growing in power and gradually establishing a leadership role in the wake of the disintegration of the Roman Empire.

Umbria and the Marches formed a buffer zone in the middle; it was the territory that stood between Rome and the north and many of the conflicts of subsequent centuries were fought out on the region's soil. It was here, for example, that Totila, the brilliant leader of the Goths, met fierce resistance in his campaign to capture the prize desired by all invaders: Rome itself.

Moreover, it was the Church, in the person of the bishops of Todi, Orvieto, Spoleto and Perugia, which led the struggle against the Goths. At Perugia, **Bishop Ercolano** galvanised his flock into withstanding a seven-year siege; towards the end he even ordered the last remaining sheep in the city to be flung over the walls to demonstrate to the Goths that Perugia still had ample food supplies. He lost the final battle and was beheaded for his pains, though miraculously the head was later found rejoined to the body.

At Spoleto, Bishop Giovanni led a heroic battle against Totila and the people of Todi, led by Bishop Fortunato, actually succeeded in holding Totila at bay for long enough for him to decide that the prize was not worth the effort. It was in Umbria, too, that Totila finally met his end, killed beneath the walls of Gualdo Tadino by the Roman commander, Narses, in AD552.

The Church, then, was a growing military force and it was an Umbrian, **St Benedict** (born in Norcia in AD480), who did more than anyone to help it achieve the dominant role it was to play in European politics over the next thousand years. St Benedict founded the first western monastic communities, and gave his followers a Rule, a disciplined structure for living, based on work, study and prayer. Without intending to do so, he not only ensured the continuity of civilisation during the dark years of the barbarian plunderers, he also laid the foundations for the economic power base of the Church; Benedictines throughout Italy and Europe quietly went about their business of establishing monasteries, taming the wilds by their labour, building churches, copying and disseminating manuscripts – and the result of all this diligence was the accumulation of substantial land holdings and wealth.

Such was the influence of the Benedictines that another set of northern invaders, the **Lombards**, eventually took up their example and adopted Christianity. The Lombards were Germanic tribesmen from the Danube valley who conquered large tracts of Italy in the wake of the Goths. Spoleto was made the capital of a sizeable principality, covering much of southern and eastern Umbria and of the Marches. This administrative unit was governed by a Duke (from dux, or leader) and divided into smaller feudal territories, each ruled by a warrior who owed allegiance to the Duke.

Pope Gregory the Great, himself the biographer and great admirer of St Benedict, was instrumental in converting the Lombards to Christianity. He sent missionaries to work amongst them, just as he sent St Augustine to convert the English. One of the abbeys founded by the Lombards – San Pietro in Valle, dating to AD720 – still survives in the wilds of the Valnerina in southern Umbria.

The Holy Roman Empire

Later popes, however, were none too happy with the presence of the Lombards on Italian soil. Lacking the resources to expel them without external aid, Pope Stephen II sought an alliance with the Franks and their leader, Pepin the Short. First Pepin, and then his son **Charlemagne**, took up the Papal cause. Charlemagne was so effective in defeating the enemies of the Church – not just the Lombards, but also the Saxons and Bavarians north of the Alps – that he was honoured with the title of Holy Roman Emperor and crowned in Rome in AD800 by Pope Leo III.

Pope Leo no doubt saw no harm in bestowing this title on such a powerful and obliging ally, and Charlemagne himself seems to have regarded the title as no more than honorific. Not so his successors, for they claimed that, as heirs of the ancient Roman emperors, they had the right to exercise territorial power in Italy. Successive popes countered with the claim that the first Christian emperor, **Constantine the Great**, had bequeathed territorial power to the Church. They produced a document, the so-called Donation of Constantine, to prove their case.

Dante was later to claim that all the troubles of Italy could be laid at the door of Constantine's bequest (the poet clearly did not see the document for the forgery that it was). For three centuries the rival claims of Church and Empire was pursued, with Europe-wide ramifications. Amongst the many issues at stake was the question of primacy: the Emperor claimed the right to appoint the Pope; the Pope countered by arguing that only he had the right to anoint and crown the Emperor, and so the argument went round and round.

That particular debate resulted in victory for the Church and a temporary truce after the signing of the Concordat of Worms in 1122. Then came Frederick Hohenstaufen, known as Barbarossa, crowned Holy Roman Emperor in 1152 and determined to settle the territorial issue. He invaded Italy and, as usual, Umbria and the Marches bore the brunt of his attack. Those cities, like Spoleto, that did not acknowledge his claims, were destroyed. Those that took Barbarossa's side found themselves saddled with tyrannical governors: in Assisi's case, Conrad of Urslingen, who built the Rocca Maggiore in 1174.

With the death of Barbarossa in 1190, Innocent III, one of the most powerful of the medieval popes, set out to exploit the anti-imperial feelings that had been generated by men like Urslingen, and he succeeded in re-establishing a measure of papal control during the 18 years of his reign (1198–1216). Then came Frederick II, grandson of Barbarossa, who attempted to reassert the territorial claims of the Emperor between 1212 and his death in 1246, and who very nearly succeeded in creating a strong, unified Italy under his control.

Frederick II blamed St Francis for his ultimate failure to break the power of the Church once and for all; not the saint personally so much as the effect that he and the Franciscan order had had in rekindling the spirit of the Church. Yet the truth is that, by this stage, the cities of Umbria and the Marches were beginning to strive towards complete independence, and were no longer content to side with either the Emperor or the Pope.

Those cities that had supported Frederick II's claims had been granted a measure of self determination, under the overall control of imperial administration. Some citizens wanted more than this: in fact, nothing less than total autonomy. Thus it was that the cities of Umbria and the Marches, as well as those further afield, became divided against each other.

The Guelphs and the Ghibellines

The terms Guelph and Ghibelline are used to denote the factions of this age, the supporters of the Pope and Emperor respectively. At another level the terms can be seen as political labels: the Guelph party was essentially made up of the rising middle class of merchants, bankers and members of the trades guilds, whose wealth was growing and with it a desire for greater control over public affairs. They supported the Pope because, temporarily at least, the papal cause seemed to offer the only hope of release from the imperial yoke. By contrast, the Ghibellines represented the old feudal aristocracy, equally interested in independence from external control, but not in a broad-based city democracy. For them, allegiance to the Emperor was a small price to pay for maintaining a virtual autocracy within the sphere of their own city state.

As a consequence, there was tension at every level in medieval Umbria and the Marches: between the superpowers of Church and Empire; between factions who nominally supported one or the other cause; between merchants and aristocracy; between rival families, many of whom maintained private armies which they deployed against each other in the struggle for city control; and between individual city states, each seeking to extend its sphere of influence and control.

Pilgrims visiting Assisi, birthplace of St Francis

Against this background of civil strife it is remarkable that the cities of Umbria and the Marches nevertheless flourished. During the 13th and 14th centuries, nearly all the important public buildings that grace the region's cities to this day – the cathedrals and town halls – were begun or completed. Nearly every city produced its constitution, with provisions for rates and taxation that enabled water supplies to be provided and palaces built for the various government functions: for the general councils, for the executives (the *priori*), for the *podestà*, the chief executive and judge, and for the Capitano del Popolo, the head of the city's army-cum-police force.

The cities prospered, even if the ideals of self-government represented by these buildings were frequently subverted by powerful families and individuals who were well able, in these troubled times, to establish their own authority in return for the security provided by their personal armies.

In the end there was no definitive and decisive end to the centuries-old struggle between Pope and Emperor. The papacy was in the ascendant and, in a show of might, **Innocent IV** sent his agent and viceroy, the Spanish Cardinal Albornoz, to assert Papal authority in central Italy. With Spoleto as his headquarters, Albornoz built the powerful Rocca, along with numerous other fortresses in the region, as much to tame the growing independence of the cities as to repel imperial troops. But, by then, the character of the papacy was also changing: after a quarrel between Pope Boniface and King Philip of France over Church taxation, the French ensured that the next pope – **Clement V** – was a Frenchman, and he made Avignon, not Rome, the papal headquarters, where it remained for much of the 14th century.

The city states

Now relatively free of external control, Umbria and the Marches began to fragment into scores of city states. Some were governed by powerful families which, having established authority over one city, set out to conquer smaller, weaker neighbours. This process was assisted by the bands of foreign mercenaries who, with the ending of the Hundred Years' War in 1360, flooded south to internecine Italy where they found ample opportunity to continue their calling. Led by so-called *condottieri*, these armies were prepared to fight for anyone willing to pay their price.

The *condottieri* were, in the beginning, undisciplined thieves who used brute force to exact whatever price they desired from helpless victims, attacking easy targets, such as small farms and undefended abbeys. The Church condemned them as 'a multitude of rogues of different nations . . . blackmailing and torturing anyone from whom they have hopes of ransom money'; yet it was not above employing *condottieri*, including the Englishman Sir John Hawkwood, leader of the notorious White Company, to fight on its behalf.

In time, however, the mercenaries became better organised and developed a highly stylised form of warfare. As Machiavelli, and other contemporary observers report, battles became ritual engagements. Any horseman who found himself in danger would surrender, pay the ransom and live to fight another day. Where two cities hired rival *condottieri* to settle a dispute, the mercenaries would agree the outcome amongst themselves and then put on a battle for the sake of their paymasters, reducing warfare to the level of contemporary wrestling, full of sound and fury but signifying nothing.

The *condottieri* were bound to their temporary employers by no other ties than money. Eventually, however, a new type of mercenary leader emerged – native Italians who were interested in conquest and rule. One of this new breed of men, Francesco Sforza, was instrumental in bringing about the relative peace that came to northern and central Italy in the 15th century. Having conquered Milan and established himself as Duke of the city, he persuaded other powerful cities and republics, such as Florence and Venice, and several smaller city states to form a defensive league, for mutual defence against attack either by foreigners or by neighbouring predators. The creation of the Italian League in 1455 not only resulted in a degree of unusual stability, it also meant that financial resources, previously soaked up by the employment of the *condottieri*, could now be used elsewhere.

The Renaissance

One result of the new stability was a flood of artistic commissions, as guilds, city governments and powerful families sought embellishments for their palazzi, guild chambers and churches. Painters, architects, sculptors, woodworkers and bronze casters were suddenly in demand and never short of lucrative work.

In Umbria and the Marches there were patrons rich enough to attract the leading artists of the day, and it has to be admitted that nearly all the region's greatest works of art were produced by outsiders, especially Florentines: the frescoes of **Cimabue** and **Giotto** in Assisi, and those of **Benozzo Gozzoli** in Montefalco, celebrating the life of St Francis; **Fra Filippo Lippi's** *Life of the Virgin* in Spoleto; the woodwork of the Duke's Library in Urbino, possibly designed by Botticelli. Another outsider, **Luca Signorelli** (born in Cortona), was responsible for the region's most singular work, the unique Last Judgement frescoes in Orvieto Cathedral, and it was a Sienese architect, **Maitani**, who gave that cathedral its outstanding form and sculpture.

Of locally born artists, the most productive were **Matteo da Gualdo** (1430–1503), born in Gualdo Tadino, **Nicola Alunno** (1430–1502) of Foligno and **Lo Spagna** (1450–1528) who, despite his name (the Spaniard), may have been born in Umbria of Spanish parents. Their works are typical of the Umbrian school in that, though they adopted the new techniques of drawing, modelling and colouration developed by Florentine painters, their art remains primarily religious and devotional: saint's lives and Madonnas are the primary subject matter.

Masolino da Panicale's 'Virgin and Child' in San Fortunato church, Todi, is a typical Umbrian school painting

For that pagan, classical element which is so much a part of the best Renaissance art, we have to look to **Perugino** (1445–1523), born in Città della Pieve, and **Pintoricchio** (1454–1513), born in Perugia. Perugino's great work, the frescoes of the Collegio del Cambio in Perugia, follow the route mapped out by humanist scholars seeking to fuse classical and Christian teaching.

In Florence artists were eventually to break free of religious subject matter altogether, to paint realistic portraits of living men and women, to create complex allegories of Spring, to portray Venus, Neptune and other pagan deities, to rediscover the nude and the equestrian statue. Perugino never went quite so far, though his preoccupation with the landscapes of his native Umbria demonstrates a desire to celebrate earthly delights. His extraordinary ability to create delicate lighting effects, the morning sunlight suffusing the dewy hills and fields of Umbria, and the lively details of trees and streams, make his frescoes satisfying to the modern eye, no longer attuned to the nuances of purely religious art.

Pintoricchio was, after studying under Perugino, even more a master of the rural landscape, filling his scenes in the church of Santa Maria Maggiore in Spello (painted at the same time as Perugino was working on the Collegio del Cambio) with scores of incidental vignettes: ploughmen at work in the fields, walled cities, travellers on horseback, people grouped in casual conversation, oblivious to the main events of the pictorial narrative.

From the mid-16th century art became considerably more timid and more academic in Umbria and the Marches than elsewhere in Italy. This has been blamed, perhaps with some justice, on the control which the Church began, once again, to exercise from this time on.

The resurgence of papal power

With steady and determined purpose, successive popes eventually succeeded in achieving the territorial control over Umbria and the Marches that they had so long sought. Sometimes all they had to do was wait: cities like Gubbio and Urbino were simply ceded to the pope when the last of the ruling delle Rovere family died without an heir. Sometimes the pope found a suitable opportunity to intervene when dynasties collapsed as a result of feuding and vendettas.

In Perugia, for example, the Baglioni had systematically clawed their way to power, from the end of the 14th century, by means of conspiracy and assassination, eliminating other families, like the Oddi, until they effectively controlled the city. They then went through a series of strategic alliances, cemented by marriage, to extend their sphere of influence well beyond the boundaries of Perugia.

One such marriage alliance was celebrated in the city in AD1500, when Astorre Baglioni wedded Lavinia Colonna, of the powerful Roman family, and all the Baglioni gathered to celebrate the event. Grifonetto Baglioni decided that this would provide an admirable opportunity to eliminate every one of his relatives at a stroke, leaving him sole ruler of the city and its domains. It was an ill-conceived plan that was bound to go wrong, given the sheer numbers involved, but Grifonetto almost succeeded. Matarazzi, the historian of this event, known as the *gran tradimento*, the great betrayal, described 'a hundred bodies heaped in the piazza in front of the cathedral, cut down by Grifonetto's hired assassins'.

Three members of the family survived and, remarkably, they clung on to power for forty years before the killing of the Papal Legate gave Pope Paul III the opportunity he needed. He sent an army of 10,000 to destroy everything the Baglioni owned and built the forbidding Rocca Paolina on the ruins of their palaces.

By such means, the cities of Umbria and the Marches were, one by one, slowly absorbed so that, by the beginning of the 17th century, they were no longer independent but merely components of the Papal State, an entity that took in all of central Italy, with the exception of Tuscany, which remained under the rule of the Medici family. For the next two centuries – they have been called the dullest period in Italian history – the region slumbered, disturbed only now and then by earthquakes, or rumblings from Rome, which unleashed bands of zealous counter-Reformationary architects to remodel and ruin so many of the region's churches and cathedrals.

Napoleon and the unification of Italy

The next challenge to papal power came, once again, from north of the Alps, in the person of the Emperor Napoleon. He invaded in 1796 and, the following year, signed a peace treaty in the Marches' town of Tolentino with representatives of Pope Pius VI. The treaty gave Napoleon the pick of the artistic treasures of Italy, which he carried back to Paris, and left Italy nominally a republic under French control.

French rule was brief and the region reverted to papal rule after the collapse of the Napoleonic regime and the 1815 Vienna Congress. Nevertheless, under Napoleon, peninsular Italy had been united for the first time since the Roman era and there was a growing desire for this state of affairs to be made permanent. Theories abounded as to how unity might be achieved: some proposed the revival of the constitution of the ancient Roman Republic, others a United Kingdom of Italy, and others a federated Italy with the Pope as President.

The actual unification of Italy took several decades of struggle to achieve, with numerous local rebellions against the Church and its foreign allies, the Austrians. Many of the streets and squares of modern Italy are named after the heroes of this struggle – **Mazzini**, **Cavour** and, above all, Giuseppe **Garibaldi**, the brave leader of the nationalist army who learned guerrilla tactics as a mercenary in South America and took on the might of the Austrian army aided by a small number of partisans.

The struggle, beginning with the first Italian War of Independence in 1848, took 22 years to reach a conclusion. Perugia was in the forefront of the rebellion against Church rule and Pius IX, in a last act of brutal repression, sent an army of the Swiss Guard to quell the city in 1859. They did so with such carnage that the event is still remembered as 'the massacre of Perugia'. The following year, Garibaldi's troops entered the city and this time the Swiss Guard barely escaped massacre at the hands of the liberated Perugians.

In November of the same year, the new provincial boundaries of Umbria and the Marches were established and the following year both provinces became members of the new United Kingdom of Italy. True unification was not finally achieved until 1870, the year in which Rome itself, the Pope's last stronghold, protected by French troops, finally fell to the Italian army.

The 20th century

From this time on, Umbria and the Marches became quiet backwaters of the new kingdom. Development in the 20th century has been most intense at the margins: the Adriatic coast and southern Umbria, especially around Terni, have the greatest concentration of industry, and hence suffered the heaviest bombing by the Allies in World War II. They then benefitted from Marshall Plan aid and rebuilt their economies while the agricultural regions at the heart of the two provinces went into rapid decline.

The result was mass emigration out of the region as the children of peasant farmers sought a better life in the industrial cities of the north, and further afield. Writers visiting the region in the 1950s record their sense of delight at discovering a people and a way of life untouched by the modern world, though that way of life was far from Arcadian for the people themselves. Only in the last thirty years has prosperity returned, the consequence of road building projects (still under way) that now link central Umbria and the mountains of the Marches to the rest of Italy.

The improved transport infrastructure has brought with it the opportunity to distribute the region's wines, cheeses, hams and truffle products to a wider market. It has also brought a large increase in the number of visitors, and a growing number of second home owners from Rome and further afield; near ruinous farmhouses and derelict city tenements are now being snapped up and converted by an ever-more mobile and prosperous European population, and the region which was once so isolated and characterful is slowly becoming more cosmopolitan, changing, as is all of Europe, as we head towards the uncharted waters of political and economic union.

3. FOOD AND WINE

Food

You do not have to be rich to eat well in Italy's heartland, unless you are determined to feast on truffles every day. The food of the region is homely and inexpensive, based on a range of simple and fresh ingredients, prepared without fuss or elaboration.

Indeed, you can do no better than heed the local saying: *piu se spenne, peggio se magna* (the more you spend, the less well you eat). With a few notable exceptions, the region's restaurateurs have no flair for the kind of dish that has been popularised by chefs of the nouvelle cuisine school, with their complex reductions, subtle combinations of flavours and fussy decoration. In a more expensive ristorante, where such tricks are imitated, you will usually eat half as well, for twice the cost, than in a simpler *trattoria* or *osteria*.

The produce

The region is blessed with an abundance of fresh and wholesome foods. The stock of an *alimentari* (grocer) or market stall may look familiar but the flavour and fragrance of the tomatoes, peaches, grapes, bread and sweet black olives, marinated in olive oil, wild thyme, garlic and orange peel, are far from commonplace.

Why do these simple foods taste so good? In part it is because, in this rural backwater of Italy, much of the food is produced by smallholders, growing fruit, vegetables and olives and rearing pigs and hens primarily for their own consumption and selling the surplus in the market or direct to small retailers. It is organically produced because the local farmers know no other method. The scale of their production is too small and the cost of sprays and fertilisers too great to justify intensive, chemical-based agriculture.

The food is supplied fresh, picked from the fields the day before it is sold. The fruits ripen naturally in the sunshine, which concentrates the flavours. Our age is becoming habituated to the bland tastes of fruit picked weeks before it is ripe and chilled until required by the supermarkets, of tomatoes grown in water under artificial light, of tasteless deep-frozen fish and meat that has not aged. The producers of Umbria and the Marches are largely ignorant of such techniques, and every self-respecting housewife shops daily, to ensure that the food she serves is fresh.

With ingredients so good the region has developed a style of cooking that involves minimal preparation and little artifice. Salads are simple yet nourishing and colourful. The local version of the Italian staple, pasta, is rustic and honest, rolled and pulled out by hand, rather than extruded through a machine. 'Macaron fatt in casa' indicates that the pasta is home-made, and the best variety is umbrici, a fat form of spaghetti, served with wild mushrooms, olive paste or (for a hefty supplement) mashed or grated truffle.

The same is true of meat and fish; characteristically they are simply grilled over the embers of a wood fire. The use of sweetly scented chestnut or vine branches imparts a wonderful flavour to the food, as does the pure virgin olive oil that is brushed over the lamb, rabbit, trout or chicken before it is placed on the grill.

But these are dishes that you would eat at the end of the day, when work is over, for such hearty food, taken too early and accompanied by a robust wine, would prostrate even the strongest of constitutions.

Breakfast

The day begins, as everywhere in Italy, with a strong dose of caffeine intended to shock the weary system into wakefulness. The breakfast (colazione) served in most hotels rarely has the desired effect, consisting as it usually does of caffe latte – white coffee – made with weak coffee and warmed-up milk and served with the tired remains of yesterday's bread.

The local bar will provide a much more effective range of kick-starters: strong black espresso (ask for caffe lungo if you need a double dose) or cappuccino – so called because the frothy white milk poured on top of the espresso resembles the white cowls of the Franciscan Capuchin friars. Sweet-toothed coffee imbibers, who have ceased to care about their weight, will munch into a cornetto, similar to a croissant, while they stand by the bar scanning the newspapers, and nobody lingers for very long.

Lunch: picnic fare

Lunch (pranzo) used to be the main meal of the day, taken at leisure and followed by a siesta. That was in the days when work in the fields began before dawn, so that by noon you would already have put in seven or eight hours of back-breaking work. The hottest hours of the day were spent indoors, out of the dangerous intensity of the midday sun. Modern factory and office hours mean that lunch is now a much shorter break, though in rural areas you will still find that nobody stirs out of doors between the hours of noon and 3pm.

There are numerous options if you do not want a formal lunch. Shops selling pizza and panini, thick sandwiches filled with cheese, tomatoes, salami or prosciutto are common in the larger towns and cities. Most bars serve similar snacks as well as more unusual delicacies: crostini, perhaps, consisting of bread dribbled with olive oil, toasted and spread with a paste of olives, mushrooms, truffles or liver mashed with anchovies and capers. The region is famous, too, for *porchetta*, a snack that is now ubiquitous in central Italy but which originated in Umbria. *Porchetta* is made by boning a whole suckling pig, stuffing the interior with bundles of fresh herbs – rosemary, sage, fennel and garlic – and roasting the result over a spit.

Porchetta is sold by pork butchers but, more traditionally, from open-sided mobile vans parked in the main square or a nearby side street. You can buy slices of the tender, juicy meat, or ask for it with bread – in which case you will be given a *rosetta*, a large round bread roll, filled with meat and crispy skin, sprinkled with salt and wrapped in waxed paper. This is a snack to be eaten at once, for the melting pork is best when still warm.

The local street market or an *alimentari* will supply you with all the ingredients for a lazy al fresco picnic. Apart from the staples of bread, vegetables and fruit, you will usually find a range of locally cured meats and cheeses. Norcia's famous hams (*prosciutti*) are now widely available. True Norcian ham is rosy and lean, and liked for its strong flavour, the result of feeding the pigs on acorns and sweet chestnuts. Even if they do not stock this, most grocers will offer a choice between the basic, artificially cured ham and premium products, such as the sweet *prosciutto della montagna* (from the mountains) or *al naturale* (naturally cured).

Many towns make their own *salame*, whose tastes differ according to the breed of pig used, the coarseness of the mince and the additional flavourings. In Umbria you can find the fragrant Citta di Castello salami, flavoured with fennel seeds, or the sweet liver sausage made with the addition of orange peel, pine kernels and raisins, called *mazzafegati*; this is definitely an acquired taste, especially the variety called *mazzafegati pazza*, which has chilli pepper added for extra bite. The Marches has a similar sausage made of pig's head, almonds, pine kernels and orange peel, and a pate called *ciauscula*, made with pork, herbs and wine.

Most of the local cheeses, as opposed to the ubiquitous mass-produced varieties, are made from the milk of ewes reared in the high mountain pastures. *Pecorino* is the generic name for all such cheese, which can be eaten young, when it is still mild, soft, white and crumbly, or when it has matured to a yellow hard cheese with a salty flavour as strong as that of parmesan. Norcian cheeses are aged alongside the region's hams and are supposed to be imbued with their flavour, while in the Marches you will often find that the *pecorino* is flavoured with herbs or wrapped in sweet chestnut leaves.

Dinner: eating out

If they are dining out, Italians usually arrive for the evening meal (cena) at about 8pm. Once there was a clear distinction, and a clear gradation in prices and service, between a *pizzeria*, *osteria*, *trattoria* and a *ristorante*. Now many a *pizzeria* serves a much wider range of dishes, while an *osteria* or *trattoria* may be as elegant as a *ristorante*. That elegance costs money, of course, and

Prosciutto (air-cured ham) made from wild boar on sale in Norcia, the sausage and ham capital of Umbria

Sweet pecorino cheese made from the milk of sheep grazed in the high Umbrian mountains

as a rough rule of thumb you can assume that the smarter the decor the higher the prices are likely to be – without the food necessarily being any better than in a cheaper establishment.

In the simpler restaurants the prices per dish will usually include service charges (if so, the menu will say *servizio compreso*), and nobody will mind if you only want a light meal. In any *trattoria* with pretensions, and in a *ristorante*, the menu will probably state *servizio non compreso*, so that you must reckon on a 15 per cent service charge on top of the bill, as well as a charge for bread and cover (*pane e coperto*). Here you will be expected to take a full meal, starting with *antipasti* or a pasta first course (*i primi*) and followed by a main course (*i secondi*) of fish or meat with salad or vegetables. The dessert course (*i dolci*) has become optional in this more health-conscious age and is usually skipped in favour of coffee or an ice cream.

The waiters should not, but usually do, expect to be tipped as well.

If you want value for money and honest cooking, always seek out the places where the local people eat with their families. Be suspicious of anywhere that offers a *menu turistico*, for it suggests lack of local patronage and is probably catering for the tastes of visitors who have set ideas about what constitutes Italian food (spaghetti and veal). On the other hand, good establishments will often offer a *menu degustazione*, consisting of the best seasonal dishes at a fixed price – but beware the little asterisks that denote a supplement for certain dishes, especially those involving truffles.

Truffles

Truffle (*tartufo*) is most abundant in late autumn and late winter, though you will find them on the menu at all times of year in the main market centres: around Spoleto, the Valnerina, Norcia and Scheggio in Umbria, and the Metauro valley in the Marches. Out of season the truffles will have been preserved by freezing, canning or vacuum packing, with an inevitable loss of flavour.

Black truffles are the most common and least expensive, and are usually grated as a flavouring over pasta dishes or used as a garnish for just about everything. The rare, more expensive bianchetto, the white truffle, has a much more pronounced fragrance and a little goes a long way; for a truffle-flavoured omelette it is possible even to omit the truffle since burying the truffle amongst the eggs for several hours is sufficient for the perfume to penetrate to the egg, even through the shell.

Again, white truffle is usually served as a sauce ingredient for pasta, sometimes combined with wild mushrooms, mashed olives or garlic, or in an omelette, which may also include cheese and prosciutto.

Truffles are, of course, not the only form of edible fungus that you will find on the autumn menu. All kinds of wild mushrooms find their way into pasta sauces, perhaps combined with herbs and bacon, but the king of the funghi is the meaty *porcini*, best enjoyed on its own, fried in butter and garlic.

Game

Autumn also marks the beginning of the official game season, when you are much more likely to find wild boar, hare, rabbit, pheasant and partridge on the menu. There seems to be no closed season for wild pigeon, and you will find this everywhere, cooked according to the local recipe. In Gubbio they make a sauce, after casseroling the pigeon for several hours, and serve it with pasta (*taglierini al ragù in bianco di piccione*). Perugians serve their pigeons with black olives and roast them (*piccione alla Perugino*). In Assisi they are stuffed with herb and garlic-flavoured lard, wrapped in bacon (*pancetta*) and casseroled in wine. A dish of pigeon stewed with root vegetables is common all over Umbria and in the Marches they stuff the body cavity with minced pork and chicken livers before roasting with bacon until the breast is just pink.

These dishes are as elaborate as any you will find in the region, and their robust flavours are an adequate distraction from, and remedy against, the winter's cold. More usually, especially in summer, meat is simply spit-roasted or grilled with a basting of oil and meat juices. Lamb, and sometimes goat, is the ubiquitous year-round staple, served plain and unadorned (*alla cacciatore* – hunter's style) or stuffed with herbs before grilling over the embers of a wood fire (*alla griglia*).

Fish

If game is characteristic of the colder months, fish begins to come into its own with the season of Lent, and continues to be enjoyed through the summer. Umbria, the only Italian province that lacks a sea coast, nevertheless has clean, fast-flowing rivers that yield wild trout and crayfish (both a speciality of restaurants in the Valnerina). Lake Trasimeno is the source of eels (*anguille*), pike (*luci*) and carp (*carpe*), usually served in a tomato sauce or fried as a mixture in olive oil and wine (*tegamaccio*).

At least one restaurant in Gubbio (the Fornace di Mastro Giorgio) serves Adriatic fish (on Thurs and Fri only) but in general you have to travel to the coastal villages of the Marches for shellfish, prawns, squid, lobster, fresh anchovies and sardines, and the twenty or so varieties of larger fish that are either served deep fried (*fritto misto*) or simply grilled. The Adriatic coast is equally renowned for fish soup (*brodetto*). Soup is perhaps a misnomer for what can be a hearty casserole, including many different fish varieties and flavourings, and every restaurant has its own jealously guarded recipe.

Pulses

Pulse foods are not eaten quite so much as in neighbouring Tuscany (where their fondness for bean stews has earned Tuscans the nickname *mangiafagioli* – bean eaters) but the tiny brown lentils grown around Castellucio have a special place in the calendar, as well as being deliciously sweet. Eaten on New Year's Eve, it is believed that the more you consume the more you will prosper in the year ahead. Around Castellucio and Norcia you can eat them the year round, usually boiled with garlic, celery and bacon and served with plump pork sausages.

Desserts

Anyone with a sweet tooth will be more than amply served by the choice of *dolci* available in most restaurants, but few of them will be special to Umbria or the Marches. Traditionally, sweets and pastries are reserved for religious festivals – Christmas, the pre-Lent carnival, Easter and saints' days. Most typical of the region are the various tarts and cakes made with pine kernels and dried fruits: Perugia has its *serpentone*, snake-like pastry rolls filled with chopped nuts, fruits and honey, while Assisi puts similar ingredients into a brioche, flavoured with cinnamon. Sweet *tagliatelle*, eaten cold with chopped walnuts and cinnamon, is common in Umbria, while the Marches' equivalent is ravioli stuffed with cinnamon, lemon and liqueur-flavoured ricotta cheese.

Wine

In the wine league, Umbria is usually regarded as a poor relation to neighbouring Tuscany, the region that produces the noble Chianti wines. By comparison, the white wines of **Orvieto** have a down-market image. Some 16 million bottles of the dry white Orvieto wine are produced annually and exported the world over, so the mass-market image is partly deserved, but to dismiss all the wines of Orvieto as utilitarian, for everyday drinking but not for special occasions, would be a mistake.

After all, the Antinori family, whose Tuscan estates produce some of that region's best wines, also produce Orvieto of quality, a fuller-bodied wine than the more anaemic *secco*. The Antinori are not alone: Barberini, Bigi and Decugnano dei Barbi are all producers of trustworthy Orvieto, and you should look for their names on the wine list. The words Orvieto Classico, by the way, are not necessarily an indication of superior quality; *classico*, attached to the name of any wine, simply denotes that the product comes from the region's long-established vineyards.

Orvieto wines today are very different to those traditionally produced. Until the late 1960s, Orvieto was a sweet and fragrant golden wine, produced (like Sauternes) by allowing the fungus known as *muffa nobile* (noble rot) to reduce the water content of the grape and concentrate the sugars. The switch to drier wines was a deliberate, and successful, marketing strategy, but several producers are now reviving the old style of wine, known generically as *abboccato* or *amabile*. If you are interested in trying this, look for **Pourriture Noble**, produced by Ducagnano dei Barbi, or **Vigneto Orzalume**, produced by the Bibi estates.

Apart from Orvieto, most of Umbria's wines come from vineyards planted in the hills between Perugia and Lake Trasimeno. The **Torgiano** DOC (the DOC classification simply guarantees that the wine does come from the specified region) was established after World War Two by the leading viticulturalist, Dr Giorgio Lungarotti, and produces some of Umbria's best wines. Look for the Lungarotti label on the full-bodied **Rubesco** or the smooth white **Torre di Giano**. The same estate produces one of Italy's greatest aged wines: **Rubesco Riserva** spends three years in the barrel and six years in the bottle before it is considered ready to drink. Enjoyable wines – red, white and rosé – are produced by the Colli di Trasimeno and Colli Perugini DOCs, as well as the relatively new Colli Altotiberini DOC, a region established as recently as 1980 by planting the hills of the Tiber valley around Citta di Castello. From the Montefalco DOC comes one of Italy's more unusual wines: **Sagrantino Passito** is bitter-sweet with an intense blackberry fragrance and is, perhaps, best reserved for the end of a meal, after a bottle of the same region's **Montefalco Rosso**, a velvety red wine, best drunk young.

Verdicchio is the Marches' equivalent of Orvieto, a light white wine produced in quantity and traditionally sold in amphorae or carboys rather than bottles. The crisp delicacy of Verdicchio at its best makes an excellent accompaniment to the region's seafood dishes. Leading producers are seeking to improve the quality of their wine and the Verdicchio from the Castelli di Jesi DOC, now sold in bottles, has a strength and flavour comparable to Muscadet.

Few other Marches' wines are well known outside the region and the consequence is that even the finest are relatively inexpensive. Young white wines, light enough to be drunk at lunch time without leaving you incapacitated for the afternoon, are **Bianchello del Metauro**, **Falerio del Colli Ascolani** and **Bianco del Colle Maceratesi**. The reds, such as **Rosso Piceno** and **Rosso Conero**, are also intended to be drunk young and fruity (within four years of the vintage), but some producers have discovered that they age well, and you may occasionally find the fuller bodied riserva on the wine list.

Finally, as an alternative to *grappa* or any of the dubiously coloured liqueurs that abound in Italy, you might like to try **Vinsanto** as a dessert wine or with coffee. Though it is not unique to the region, Umbrian producers – such as Lungarotti and Greco di Todi – make Vinsanto that is acknowledged to be as good as any made in Italy. Vinsanto is made by drying the grapes before pressing, traditionally by the fireside in order to give the resulting juice a slightly smoky flavour, and then fermenting the result in tiny barrels for several years. Vinsanto tastes like madeira or medium-dry sherry and the name – holy wine – is said to have arisen because Italian priests are very fond of it!

4. TOURING THE REGION

This guide has been written in the form of an itinerary, covering the most rewarding sights of Umbria, the Marches and San Marino. Even so, it is not restrictive: you would need at least a month to do the itinerary comprehensively, so, if you are limited to a week or fortnight, there is plenty of scope for deciding what to see and what to omit, depending on your personal interests.

You might also want to try different routes, armed with the Touring Club Italiano's 1:200,000 scale map of Umbria/Marche. I have tried to recommend the most scenic routes, principally on minor roads where you will scarcely see another car, but with restless children or limited time, you may prefer the more direct main roads to the slow, twisting and often vertiginous mountain passes.

How to travel

The itinerary has been written on the assumption that you will be touring by car – the only practical way of seeing much of the region, since only the major cities are accessible by railway and even then – be warned – the railway stations are often well out of town, with a long steep climb to reach your destination.

The region is accessible from three international airports – Pisa, Rome and Bologna. Of the three, Pisa is best because it is then just over 160 kilometres by autostrada to the region's most important destinations – Assisi and Perugia. The autostrada passes through attractive Tuscan countryside, with the option of breaking the journey at Florence or Arezzo.

I have also found that Pisa airport suffers less from those industrial disputes that can ruin a holiday. Perhaps for that reason, plus the number of foreigners who now have second homes in Tuscany, flights to Pisa are heavily used, and if you want to save money by taking a charter flight in summer, you should book as early in the year as possible.

The journey up from Rome is about the same distance – 176 kilometres to

Perugia – but passes through a heavily industrialised region of Italy. The merit of Bologna is that flights are not so heavily booked so you can make a relatively late decision when to go, and the autostrada is only a matter of yards from the airport. This takes you to San Marino – a distance of some 290 kilometres – from where you could follow this book's itinerary in reverse, or cross the mountains to enter Umbria down the Via Flaminia from the North.

When to go

Deciding when to visit Umbria and the Marches is not easy if you are in the fortunate position of having a choice. I have toured the region in all four seasons, and discovered that each season has its distinct merits.

Winter

Visiting in winter, when few other tourists were about, it was a delight to wander through the splendid rooms of the Palazzo Ducale in Urbino, and stand in Duke Frederico's study admiring Botticelli's delightful intarsia-work panelling entirely alone. I was accompanied only by the friendly gallery attendant, who went before me turning on the lights, as if I were the Duke himself, attended by a servant, on a tour of inspection.

To the pleasures of solitude, winter also adds clear skies and sunny days so that the views, unobscured by summer's haze, can be spectacular. This is the professional photographer's favourite season, when the shadows throw the sculpture on church façades into deep relief, and the hilltop cities are crisply outlined against blue skies. Shopkeepers also have more time to stop and chat, and you will see much more of the ordinary life of the region than in the busier summer months.

In winter, museum opening hours are slightly more restrictive, souvenir shops are closed (a plus, you might think), as are some hotels and restaurants. On the other hand, you will benefit from cheaper flights and car hire and many hotels offer discounted room, dinner and breakfast packages.

The mountainous region north of Norcia may be an exception to these generalisations, very much depending on the amount of snow. Skiers, in search of uncrowded slopes, have begun to discover this wild and beautiful part of the Apennines, much to the benefit of the local economy. On the other hand, a series of mild, snowless winters has almost killed this trade in its infancy. If there is deep snow, the hotels of Norcia and environs will be full in winter – if not, there will be substantial discounts on hotel rooms.

Spring

Any time from the last frosts of March to early June – is the best time to go for wildflowers and for the wonderful sight of the region's rocky rivers in full spate, as the snows melt on the mountain tops. Then there is a sense of freshness and renewal in the air, the hillsides are brilliant with the bright green of trees putting on their new foliage and the skies are that limpid blue which you see in Perugino's frescoes and paintings.

Assisi celebrates the arrival of spring with the festival of Calendimaggio, when everyone in the town puts on medieval costume and joins in the colourful parades that take place between 29 April and 1 May.

The other important traditional springtime festival in the region is Gubbio's Corsa dei Ceri, the Race of the Candles, celebrated every 15 May as it has been since 1154. The phallic shape of the three candles, octagonal structures of wood over 6m in height, may hint at earlier, pagan fertility rites. Today the candles are surmounted by statues of St Ubaldo, the town's patron, St George and St Antony, patrons of merchants and farm workers respectively.

Three teams of Gubbians race with the weighty candles on their shoulders, from the Piazza della Signoria up the town's punishingly steep and winding streets to the doors of the Basilica of Sant' Ubaldo, on the summit of Monte Ingino, some 827m above sea level. Since there is not space enough for the teams to overtake in the narrow streets they set off at intervals and animated discussions take place at the end of the race to establish the winner – the team that demonstrated the most skill and prowess, and the one that either closed or increased the gap between themselves and their pursuers.

Elsewhere, in Panicale and Citta della Pieve, the fountains flow with wine for a day in April (the date varies), a custom which is increasingly being copied by other towns in the region, most of which have wine and food festivals in June and July.

These festivals can be enormous fun, provided that you do not expect to rise early the next day. Do not expect anything too traditional. Sponsorship usually comes from local businesses and political organisations and they, aware of the tastes of voters and consumers, usually hire dance bands and ballad crooners to entertain the crowds.

Nevertheless, these festivals provide an opportunity to see provincial Italy at its most festive and to sample good local food and wine.

Summer

At the opposite end of the scale from the rustic carnival is the cosmopolitan Festival dei Due Mondi – Festival of the Two Worlds – held in Spoleto in late June and early July. Founded by opera composer Gian Carlo Menotti in 1957, the original idea was to bring together young artists from Italy and America and it has since grown into the best music, drama, and ballet festival in Italy, an important event in the country's social, as well as cultural, calendar.

Unless you book tickets well in advance (see Useful Addresses, p.180) you will have no hope of staying in the city or of attending the principal events. You can, however, stay nearby and visit Spoleto for the unique festival atmosphere and the numerous free art exhibitions and street performances.

June and July generally bring the beginning of the mass tourism season – but Assisi, Urbino and San Marino are the major destinations of the coach-

Fisherman on Lake Trasimeno

bound tourists and you will find that the rest of Umbria and the Marches remains relatively uncrowded. In August, though, Italy itself takes a month's holiday and, ironically, some hotels and restaurants are closed. This is the time when accommodation is most difficult to find and campsites are often full – the time, too, to avoid Lake Trasimeno and Lake Piediluco, with their crowded watersports resorts and beaches.

Autumn

September and October bring the harvest and another round of festivals – in honour not just of the grape but also of the chestnut (in Piediluco), the onion (in Collemancio) and of mushrooms, especially the noble and expensive *tartufo*, the truffle.

Events centred around the truffle take place in Gubbio and Norcia, but best of all is to visit the early morning markets of Acqualagna, a major trading centre for the prized white truffles. Here you can watch envious crowds gather to examine the results of a dawn expedition with truffle hound or pig, watch

41

restaurateurs and wholesalers bargaining over prize specimens and later, perhaps, dine on a breakfast of omelettes flavoured with the thinnest of truffle
shavings. San Marino, too, offers pageantry as the Republic celebrates the
twice-yearly instalment of the two Captains Regent (1 October and 1 April).
The Captains are chosen from the 60-strong Grand Council to serve a six-
month term as State Representatives and Heads of the Executive.

Where to go

If this calendar of the region's seasonal attractions helps you to decide when
to go, the next question is where to base yourself. My own prejudices are
clear since I begin the book with Assisi. This pilgrim town has a special
atmosphere which you do not have to be religious to enjoy, and the longer
you stay the more you will grow to love Assisi, with its friendly inhabitants
and spotlessly clean flower-filled streets.

Besides, you will need to visit the basilica several times, especially in the
calm of the early morning, to appreciate fully the great fresco cycles, and the
rest of the town's attractions can scarcely be seen in a day.

From Assisi all the principal cities are accessible within a day and you will
never cease to be thrilled by the sight of the town and great basilica, bathed
in evening sunlight, as you drive back up to it at the end of a day.

Perugia, by contrast, would be the better base for anyone who demands a
livelier nightlife. The presence of the ancient University and the University
for Foreigners ensures that there is always a wide choice of activities, ranging
from discotheques to English-language films.

If, on the other hand, you want to combine sightseeing with beachside
relaxation, tennis, riding or windsurfing, you should investigate the hotels of
Passignano and Castiglione del Lago, or any of the numerous campsites that
line the shore of Lake Trasimeno between these two towns.

Once out of central Umbria the choice of hotels is more limited and rec-
ommendations are given at the end of each section.

Making the most of your time

My final words on touring concern how to get the most out of a day, bearing
in mind that nearly everything in Italy closes for two or three hours in the
early afternoon.

In summer particularly it really does pay to rise early, for church doors
open at about 7.00am and at that hour you will often be the only visitor.
Forget hotel breakfast, which so often consists of yesterday's bread and
warmed-up stale coffee, and take a reviving capuccino instead in a local bar,
along with other half-awake townspeople getting ready to go to work.

You will then have plenty of time to explore churches, in the cool of the morning, before museum doors open at 10am. The museum doors close promptly at noon, allowing an hour to shop for picnic food or rest before a restaurant lunch. If you are moving on to another town you will have the roads to yourself for a couple of hours and can find a picnic spot by driving up virtually any unmetalled road (white roads on the Touring Club Italiano's map) until you reach a tree-shaded spot with a view.

Churches and museums open again between 3pm and 4pm until 6 or 7pm. If you need money, beware: banks open only for an hour in the afternoon, usually between 3pm and 4pm. Shops will remain open until 7pm, so if you missed the early morning market you can buy dinner provisions from the stock of an *alimentari*, or grocer.

If, on the other hand, you are dining out, you will find quiet and plenty of choice at 7pm when restaurants open. Italians eat later – the tables will fill between 8 and 9pm. If you want a livelier atmosphere, you can join them and burn the candle at both ends; but then, that is what holidays are for.

5. ASSISI

At 7am Assisi is still a sleepy town. In the café just off Piazza Matteotti shirt-sleeved policemen are rousing themselves with frothy, sweetened capuccino, preparing to face another day directing chaotic traffic around the perimeter of the town and keeping vehicles out of the centre itself.

The sun has risen but Assisi, clinging to the west face of Mount Subasio, remains cool, thanks to the deep shadow cast by the peak. Nine hundred metres below, in the Vale of Spoleto, car-borne commuters are already sweating in the heat, and from Assisi the Vale is already obscured by heat haze.

One building alone in Assisi is dramatically spotlit by the sun: the Rocca Maggiore, at the highest point in the town, is always the first to receive the sun's rays.

This is the best time of day to begin a tour of Assisi – and almost the last time you can be sure of finding a parking space. Now is the time to see the great Basilica of San Francesco, before the coach-borne tourists arrive, and the best way to reach it, if you are approaching from the car parks or hotels east of the town, is to climb to the Rocca Maggiore itself, by means of the Via della Rocca.

This little-used lane follows the northern perimeter of the town walls from which the ground falls away steeply to the valley of the River Tescio. As you walk, watch the swallows launch themselves from the pink and white stone walls, built of fine-grained metamorphosed chalk, admire the grace with which the birds skim the path ahead of you and enjoy the sound of their twittering which fills the air.

From the Rocca, the Via del Colle, no more than a pathway, descends to the basilica and offers unexpected views of the major buildings of the town – the façade of the cathedral, and the Torre del Commune, the Romanesque campanile in the town's main square, framed between sculptural groups of slender cypress trees.

The path joins Via Santa Croce and descends, via a series of stone staircases, to the Via Cardinale Mery del Val. Here, suddenly after narrow medieval streets, you enter the wide grassed-over Piazza Superiore di San Francesco with its uninterrupted view down on to the west front of the basilica.

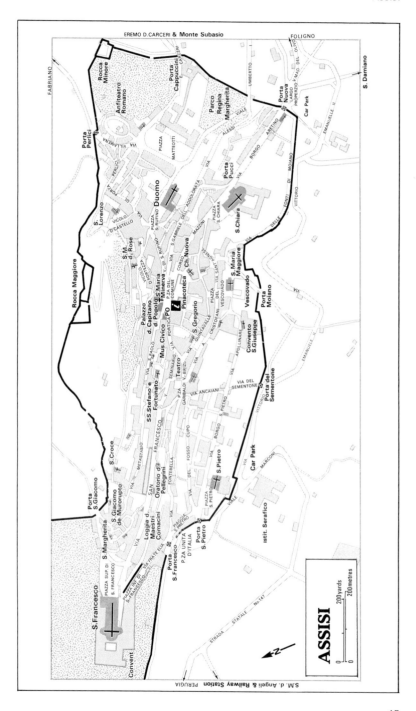

The Basilica

Down by the basilica entrance, friars in brown habits and sandals chat in the first warmth of the morning sunlight, waiting to guide parties around the echoing church. Perhaps 5000 people will pass through in the morning and the same number in the afternoon, stopping en route between Perugia and Rome to see the frescoes of Giotto and Cimabue. The friars, in explaining the frescoes and the scenes they illustrate, never fail to deliver a brief homily, drawing out the morals and universal truths in the story of St Francis.

St Francis

Ironically the saint who led a life of absolute simplicity and poverty is buried in one of the most splendid churches in Christendom. It is an often repeated cliché that the sumptuousness of this building contradicts everything that St Francis represented.

By the time of his death the Franciscan Order had already split into two camps: one that espoused the original rule of St Francis, owning nothing and sharing their alms with the needy, and those who believed that the objective of succouring the poor could be better achieved by deliberate and efficient fund raising, founded on the basis of a well-run organisation. The same arguments are familiar today as charities try to seek a balance between spending on publicity and administration and distributing the donations they receive.

Towards the end of his life St Francis was no longer Vicar General of the order he founded and the reformist wing was in the ascendancy, led by Brother Elias, one of the saint's earliest followers. Elias masterminded a campaign to ensure that St Francis would be in Assisi when he died, and would be buried here. With future canonisation a virtual certainty, Elias wanted the revenue from pilgrims who would visit St Francis's shrine. He was also determined to build a church and monastery that would serve as the worldwide headquarters of a powerful and influential order.

St Francis had never been a healthy man. His conversion to a life of preaching and contemplation resulted from a long illness at the age of 20 that frustrated his plans to become a crusader. The physical punishments he imposed upon himself – throwing himself naked in winter into a bed of roses, for example – plus the thousands of miles he travelled on foot through Italy, Spain and Egypt protected only by a coarse peasant's habit, caused his health to deteriorate further.

When St Francis fell ill in Siena, Brother Elias sent an armed escort to fetch him home and guard him from any would-be kidnappers. The strategy succeeded but when St Francis died, at the age of 45, on 4 October 1226 he was not in the Bishop's Palace in Assisi, as his supporters wished, but down in the valley on the floor of the Porziuncola, the little church around which St Francis built his first Franciscan community.

It is said that St Francis asked to be buried anonymously among the graves

The entrance to the Basilica di San Francesco, Assisi

of the poor on the Colle del Inferno, the Hill of Hell, at the western end of Assisi – so called because it was here that criminals were executed. His wish was granted, but not before Elias obtained the rocky promontory as the site of his planned new basilica. Lawyers worked out a formula whereby the Franciscans, forbidden by their rule to own property, would enjoy the rights of ownership in perpetuity while the title remained with the Pope.

Two years after his death, in 1228, Francis was canonised in a ceremony led by Pope Gregory that would have made the saint laugh at its pomp and absurdity. He had always enjoined his followers to 'beware of being sad and gloomy like hypocrites, but rather be joyful in the Lord, gay and pleasant'. According to contemporary accounts of the canonisation ceremony, after a long list of miracles attributed to St Francis had been read out the Pope and assembled cardinals were so moved to tears that their vestments were wet and the ground drenched.

Construction of the basilica began that same year, funded, in part, by the sale of indulgences that offered remission from time in Purgatory in return for hard cash. When a party of raiding Perugians tried to steal the body of St Francis, temporarily buried in the church of San Giorgio, Elias decided that the moment had come for the official funeral, rather than waiting to see the basilica completed.

The funeral took place on 25 May 1230. Vast crowds from all over Italy attended and onlookers showered the saint's coffin, drawn by two white oxen, with bouquets of wild flowers. As the cortège approached the basilica, an armed guard, organised by Elias, seized the coffin, bolted the doors and interred the body in secrecy, intending to frustrate any future saint snatchers. Not even the Pope was expecting this turn of events and the crowd was indignant at the unceremonious end to the day, but the exact location of St Francis's tomb remained undiscovered until 1818.

The building

Over the tomb Elias raised the awesome double basilica that we see today, an outstanding feat of engineering that involved building a platform out from the rocky spur at the western end of Assisi. The earliest supporting structure proved, in time, to be inadequate. The majestic series of fifty-three arches, in two tiers, that now supports the complex and gives it such a dramatic appearance when viewed from the approach roads to Assisi, was added in the 1470s to shore up the subsiding structure.

The steep fall of the hillside also made access from the west impossible, and this accounts for the orientation of the basilica, which you enter from the east, looking west to the transepts and high altar, the reverse of the usual plan.

The design of the basilica is attributed to Elias himself but, as with so many great medieval churches, the credit should probably go to the anonymous master masons who were in charge of the day-to-day work and the all-important details. They worked with the beautiful rose-pink stone that lay close to hand in Mount Subasio, fine-grained limestone, almost plastic in texture and easily carved.

The style of the exterior is a mixture of Gothic and Romanesque, with some Renaissance additions for good measure. Appearances, though, can be deceptive for the beautiful wheel window of the east façade, decorated with cosmati work, was designed by Pietro di Pietrisanta and inserted at the end of the 15th century, despite its Romanesque appearance. It is therefore later than the Gothic twin portal below or the great Romanesque bell-tower, completed in 1239, that rises behind the church.

From the upper terrace a double marble staircase descends to the Piazza Inferiore, the lower courtyard, lined on either side by graceful 15th-century colonnades whose multiple arches are too often obscured since the piazza serves as a car and coach park. The lower basilica is entered from this piazza, through the prothyrum, built in 1487, that shelters a fine Gothic portal.

In the lower basilica

The ceilings and walls of the lower basilica are covered in some of the most important medieval frescoes in Europe, but do not expect to be bowled over at once by the wealth of rich colour. It takes time for the eye to adjust to the gloom of the unlit crypt, and it is best to sit and contemplate for a while. As you do you will notice that well-prepared visitors carry powerful hand torches, as do the guides, to illuminate portions of fresco – a sensible idea. The alternative is to carry pockets full of small change to feed into the coin-operated spotlights – or just wait until somebody else pays for the lights to be turned on.

When the lower basilica was originally built, it consisted simply of the nave – which slopes downhill slightly towards the main altar – and the two transepts, together forming a cross shape. When the side chapels were added in the late 13th century, piercing through the nave walls, much of the original fresco decoration in the nave was lost. The scenes that survive, painted around 1236, are attributed to the anonymous Maestro di San Francesco. They include an endearing picture of St Francis preaching to an attentive congregation of birds.

It is almost impossible to see the remaining frescoes in chronological order without darting to and fro, so it is best to take them as they come. Thus the first chapel on the left, the Capella di San Martino, contains Simone Martini's *Scenes from the Life of St Martin*, among the last of the frescoes to be executed in the lower basilica and arguably the best.

Martini worked on the chapel from 1322 to around 1326 and was responsible for all the decorations, including the stained glass windows depicting eighteen saints and the marble decoration of the floor.

In painting the walls, Martini deliberately drew out the parallels between the lives of St Martin and St Francis. St Martin's division of his cloak in order to share it with a poor man (bottom, left-hand wall) echoes the first symbolic act of St Francis when he stripped off his clothes in renunciation of worldly possessions. In another scene (bottom right) St Martin renounces arms – as St Francis did when he gave up his intended career as a crusading soldier – and trusts, henceforth, to the protection of God – again as St Francis did when he walked into the enemy camp of Melek-el-Kamel in Egypt in order to convert the Sultan to Christianity.

Martini's frescoes are outstanding for the richness of the colour and the expressive faces of the dramatis personae. His work has been called 'sweet, lovable, gentle', and you can see these qualities even in the faces of the horses that are present in several scenes. Art critics, however, do not always apply these epithets in terms of praise and argue that his decorative work lacks energy and realism.

Crossing to the rear of the basilica, the Cappella di Sant' Antonio Abate contains the 14th-century tomb of Blasco Fernandez, Duke of Spoleto, and his son, both assassinated in 1350. A doorway from the chapel leads out into the Old Cemetery, a quiet, cypress-filled cloister. If you can find a passing friar, ask to be taken into the adjacent cloister garden for fine views of the superimposed upper and lower basilicas, shored up by flying buttresses, with further cylindrical buttresses of pink stone.

Midway down, on the right-hand side of the nave, steps lead down to the crypt in which St Francis is buried, along with four of his early followers. Here the unadorned stone walls offer nothing to please the eye but are, perhaps, more in keeping with the saint's own love of simplicity and his wishes concerning the disposal of his mortal remains. The burial crypt was rediscovered in 1818 after two months of excavation. The neo-classical superstructure built around the tomb in the 19th century was removed in 1925 when the crypt took on its present appearance.

The chapel of St Mary Magdalene

Emerging from the crypt, turn right for the last chapel before the transept, dedicated to St Mary Magdalene. The frescoes and stained glass illustrate her life and include (on the left wall) a portrait of the Bishop of Assisi, Trebaldo Pontano (1296–1329) who paid for the decoration. The frescoes are attributed to Giotto, aided by assistants. This is just one example of a contentious attribution. Some scholars have even gone as far as to suggest that Giotto never visited Assisi and that, as with the authorship of Shakespeare's plays, the credit has gone to the wrong person.

In this respect Vasari, chronicler of the *Lives of the Artists*, is not a reliable witness. He says that (after painting 32 scenes from the life of St Francis in the upper basilica):

> Giotto did some more work in the same place, but in the lower church, painting the upper part of the walls beside the high altar and all four angles of the vault above where St Francis is buried.

Today even the most partisan supporter of Giotto's genius doubts this attribution and the ceiling frescoes above the high altar are now credited, for lack of any other evidence, to an anonymous Maestro delle Vele (Master of the Vaults). They depict the apotheosis of St Francis and complex allegories of the three principles upon which the Franciscan Order was founded: Chastity, Poverty and Obedience. Chastity is portrayed as a maiden in a white tower, defended by Purity and Fortitude. In the foreground, a naked man is being washed by angels, symbolising purification. To the right, Cupid and Concupiscence are being chased away. To the left, St Francis greets three figures dressed in the habits of the Franciscans, the Poor Clares and the lay Franciscan brotherhood.

Poverty, in the next scene, is portrayed as a bride being given to St Francis in marriage. She is barefoot and walking on thorns, her way impeded by a barking dog and a scornful stone-throwing youth; St Francis, in his own barefoot wanderings, frequently encountered just such ridicule.

Finally, Obedience is portrayed as a seated figure placing a yoke on the neck of a kneeling friar, a finger at her lips to enjoin silence. A centaur in the foreground, representing unbridled passion, is being driven away.

The transepts

The left transept is decorated with scenes from the Passion of Christ. The frescoes, executed by the Sienese artist Pietro Lorenzetti around 1320, are as remarkable as any in the basilica. They seem, indeed, to anticipate the Renaissance in the realistic detailing – natural blue for the sky rather than the celestial gold of Gothic art – and the use of perspective in scenes that contain much architectural detail.

Lorenzetti's pictures are crowded with people; this only serves to highlight the scene in which the suicidal Judas hangs from a tree entirely alone. In the great Crucifixion scene, sadly mutilated in the early 16th century when an altar was set against the wall, the crowds gathered around the cross are like a chorus in Greek tragedy, their faces and attitudes providing a varied commentary on the central drama – from the jeering and brutal soldiers who are breaking the legs of the unrepentant thief to the sorrow of the majority.

Even more expressive are the faces of Christ's mourners in the Deposition scene, one in which Lorenzetti transforms Byzantine stylisation of flowing hair and drapery into a forceful symbol of the turbulent thoughts and feelings of the onlookers.

Near the Crucifixion is Lorenzetti's *Madonna and Child with St John the Evangelist*, called the Madonna of the Sunset because the tender face of the Virgin is illuminated by the rays of the setting sun as the light filters through the opposite window.

The right-hand transept contains frescoes executed by Cimabue between 1270 and 1280. Restoration has removed some of the heavy-handed overpainting that had obscured the original work of this major artist to whom Vasari attributed the revival of Italian painting. Vasari tells us that the secrets of true fresco had been lost until Cimabue learned the techniques by observing Greek artists hired to paint the Gondi Chapel in Florence.

Vasari also tells us that Cimabue 'did a small panel of St Francis . . . drawing the saint, to the best of his powers, from nature; and this was a new departure for the time'. It was indeed an innovation because medieval practice had been to paint idealised portraits, iconographic representations intended for spiritual contemplation, rather than true likenesses.

Cimabue painted another portrait here, on the right-hand vault of the right transept, where St Francis stands alongside the Virgin and Child. The likeness corresponds with the description of St Francis given by his friend and biographer, Fra Tommaso da Celano: 'rather on the small side . . . a straight, thin nose, ears jutting outward . . . slim hands with long fingers and nails . . . thin, roughly dressed.'

Other scenes in this transept attributed to Cimabue and Giotto (or his followers) illustrate events from the childhood of Christ, paralleled by miracles involving infants worked by St Francis: the little girl who survived a fall from a tower, and a small boy pulled alive from a collapsed building in Suesa. This last scene, on the end wall, is said to include portraits of Giotto (holding the boy's head) and Dante (behind him).

Nearby, on the same wall, are five saints once attributed to Simone Martini but now considered to be by an assistant, perhaps even his brother, Donato. One of the figures, the beautiful meditative female saint carrying a crucifix, may be Santa Chiara (St Clare), companion of St Francis and founder of the Poor Clares.

From the transept, steps lead up and out of the basilica into the sunlit terrace to the rear. The terrace and its cloister were built in 1474 during the reign of Pope Sixtus IV when the friary buildings were extended and the underpinning of the basilica was strengthened. Backward views reveal the lovely pink and white walls of the upper basilica. The Treasury, off the cloister, is used to house the Perkins Collection of 14th- and 15th-century paintings and a great range of vestments, chalices and reliquaries accumulated by the Franciscans over several centuries.

The upper basilica

The upper basilica forms the artistic highlight of a visit to Assisi. It is bright and well-lit compared to the basilica below and every surface is covered with colour. The plan of the basilica is simple and has remained untouched since completion in 1253: just a nave, choir, transepts and apse. Despite the simplicity and the lack of superfluous furnishings, the effect of the frescoes is so overwhelming that it takes time to find your orientation.

The apse and transepts, which you enter first, are frescoed throughout by Cimabue and his assistants. Much of this work has deteriorated beyond the point where restoration can help. The lead pigments used by the artists have oxidised to a purplish black colour, giving the frescoes the appearance of photographic negatives.

Even so, it is still worth looking closely at Cimabue's *Crucifixion*, in the left-hand (south) transept, considered to be the artist's finest work. You can see the Byzantine influence that Cimabue absorbed as a boy, playing truant from school to watch and copy the work of Greek artists, especially in the patterning of the drapery folds on the foreground figures.

The drama of the scene, however, owes nothing to the eastern tradition and shows what Cimabue was capable of achieving at the height of his powers – deliberately counterpointing the animal brutality of the crowd on the right with the grief of the onlookers on the left. The result is a dramatic symmetry in which the hands of the stone-throwing mob are mirrored by the upraised hands of Christ's grieving mother, a symmetry deliberately broken by the little kneeling figure of St Francis at the foot of the cross.

Other apocalyptic scenes by Cimabue around the apse are now almost indecipherable. Below them is the marble throne used by the Pope when he visits Assisi, flanked by wooden stalls, dated to 1491–1501, with beautiful intarsia-work portraits of Franciscan saints.

The Life of St Francis fresco cycle

Cimabue's frescoes are the prelude to the great glory of the basilica, the fresco cycle illustrating the Life of St Francis on the lower walls of the nave. It is now acceptable, once again, to attribute most of these scenes to Giotto, for art scholars have agreed on a sort of truce which acknowledges the hand of different artists in the last five scenes while allowing the remainder to be the work of the great artist who transformed the emphasis of Western art.

It is not immediately obvious why these paintings are regarded so highly, or why they were considered revolutionary in their time; so important that many of the great artists of the Renaissance, from Masaccio onwards, came to study and copy them.

At one level Giotto's claim to fame is due to his technical mastery. His colours, even today, are bright, bold, luminescent – perhaps even gaudy in some scenes. He was master, too, of draughtsmanship and used this skill to delineate expressive gestures that lend life, individuality and character to his figures. This, above all, was admired by his contemporaries, and Vasari, in his eulogistic account of Giotto's life, continually praises his powers of observation, saying that 'he was always going to nature itself for new ideas and so he could rightly claim to have had nature, rather than any human master, as his teacher.'

If, to our modern eyes, some of his figures are still lumpen, if they lack the articulation that later artists, schooled in anatomy and classical sculpture, were to achieve, we have to remember how much more lifelike his figures are than those of earlier artists. The scenes on the upper nave wall, predating the St Francis cycle and painted by Cimabue's pupils (including, perhaps, Giotto himself) offer instructive comparisons with the mature work of the artist below.

Of course, Giotto could not have found a more appropriate stimulus for his imagination than the life of St Francis. The artist who was inspired by nature must have felt kinship with the saint whose own love of the sun, the moon, the elements and all God's creatures was itself such a revolutionary concept in the 13th century.

Indeed, the idea that humanity should respect and live in balance with nature remains a highly controversial doctrine to this day, especially when attempts are made to convert sentiment into political actions. In the late Middle Ages there were no doubt many people who looked at their environment and found it beautiful, but in general nature symbolised at best a temporary world, a pale reflection of Paradise, and at worst a realm of beasts and base instincts from which a hard-won living must be derived.

In this respect Giotto's frescoes bridge the modern and the medieval imagination, fluctuating between scenes of vivid realism and scenes of demons and miraculous events; they are part biography and part hagiography.

The sequence of 28 frescoes begins on the north wall nearest the high altar. The first is set in the main square of Assisi, the Piazza del Commune, recognisable by the façade of the Roman Temple of Minerva, still standing today. Here the young St Francis, the son of a wealthy cloth merchant, is being honoured by a poor man who spreads his cloak for St Francis to walk on and predicts that he will one day be greatly venerated.

In the next scene, St Francis is depicted in the plain below Assisi, with the walled city in the background and the Benedictine monastery of Mount Subasio, later to be the saint's favourite retreat, on the hill to the right. Francis has set off on a journey, intending to join the crusaders and fight in the Holy Land. He stops to offer his costly saffron and purple cloak to a poor man that he meets along the way.

Still intent on a knightly career, we next see St Francis dreaming of a palace filled with armour – helmets and breastplates – all marked with a red cross. The meaning is unclear to St Francis who believes, at first, that God approves his military ambitions.

In the next scene St Francis prays before a crucifix in the ruined church of San Damiano, just outside the walls of Assisi (see page 67). This scene represents the turning point in the saint's life. He has suffered illness and, finding little pleasure in his old way of life, seeks clarification of his future through prayer and solitary contemplation. Christ speaks from the cross, urging Francis three times to 'Repair my house, which you see is falling into ruin.'

We need to turn to the various biographers of St Francis to fill in the events that link this and the next scene. Apparently St Francis took the injunction to 'repair my house' in its literal sense and set about repairing the fabric of San Damiano. To pay for the restoration he stole a bale of cloth from his father's warehouse and sold it.

For a month St Francis hid in a cave alongside San Damiano, praying and fasting until his father, furious at the theft and his son's apparent madness, found him, beat him and locked him up at home. Francis escaped back to San Damiano, with the help of his mother, and this time the father dragged St Francis before the Bishop of Assisi.

In the next scene, then, the apoplectic father, his face yellow, demands that Francis either returns home for good or renounces his inheritance. Francis, without hesitation, removes his clothes and hands them back to his father, raising his arms in a gesture of trust in God and renunciation of all possessions. The pious bishop covers the nakedness of St Francis with a cloak.

The next scene leaps forward in time to the year 1210 when St Francis went to Rome to seek the Pope's permission to found a new religious order. In the meantime he has spent several years as a peripatetic preacher, begging for alms and distributing them amongst the poor, and gathering around him a community of like-minded people.

Pope Innocent III hesitates. A new movement, especially one that emphasises poverty and charitable works, could be a thorn in the flesh of an extremely wealthy and powerful Church. Moreover, new movements were springing up all over Europe at this time, threatening the unity and discipline of the Church, and many of them subsequently proved to be heretical.

Again the issue is settled by a dream and in the next scene Pope Innocent lies asleep in his costly purple robes and sees a vision of a monk in a rough brown woollen habit physically holding up the collapsing church of the Lateran in Rome, a symbol of the role that St Francis will play in the revival of the original principles upon which the Church was founded.

In the next scene Giotto again decorously counterpoints the poverty and humility of the friars with the pomp and majesty of the Pope and cardinals who meet to approve the new rule of the Franciscan Order.

In the next three scenes we enter the surrealistic world of medieval myth. In the first a group of Franciscans see their leader riding through the sky in a fiery chariot. Then St Francis himself sees a series of heavenly thrones and an angel who explains that they were once occupied by Lucifer and the rebel angels but are now reserved for St Francis and his followers. Finally we see St Francis standing before the walls of Arezzo, driving out the demons that had occupied the city and goaded the inhabitants into an orgy of self-destruction.

The theme of St Francis as a pacifist continues in the next scene. After two failed attempts to reach the Moslems in North Africa, foiled by shipwreck and illness, St Francis finally set sail from the Marches port of Ancona, in June 1219, and sailed up the Nile Delta. There, in pursuit of his ambitions to convert the Moslems to Christianity, he sought an audience with Sultan Malek-al-Kamil, with whom the crusaders were at war.

It seems that the Sultan enjoyed the company of this earnest but good-humoured little friar for St Francis stayed several days as a guest in the enemy camp and emerged alive from the encounter. That much is probably historical truth, but Giotto has chosen to illustrate the more dramatic episode from the hagiographies in which St Francis walks barefoot and unharmed through a blazing fire in order to prove the truth of the Gospels to the Sultan.

In the 12th scene, perhaps not entirely by the hand of Giotti, St Francis is portrayed in an ecstasy of prayer, surrounded by a cloud and his arms outspread as he identifies with the Passion and Crucifixion of Christ. Next comes one of the most endearing of the events in the life of the saint. In 1223, just three years before his death, St Francis instituted the first Christmas crib in order to communicate the mystery and awe of the Nativity to the illiterate peasants of Greccio. Giotto has set this tableau in a church, but biographers say the re-enactment of the birth of Christ, complete with living child, ox and ass, was mounted in a cave that St Francis was then using as a hermitage. He invited local shepherds to witness the scene and they must have been as awed by the sight as any child seeing their first Christmas crib would be today. Many an Umbrian church still follows St Francis's example of mounting a living tableau.

The Miracle of the Spring, illustrated in the next scene, was considered by Vasari to be one of Giotto's most naturalistic works. He described the peasant, drinking at the stream, as 'just like a real person, desperate with thirst'. The incident illustrates the injunction of St Francis to his followers that they should own nothing and trust in God to provide for their needs. When the owner of a donkey, hired to convey the ailing St Francis, complained of thirst, the saint merely prayed and a spring gushed forth.

Scene 15, the Sermon of the Birds, is the most celebrated fresco in the cycle, despite the fact that it has lost much of its force through the deterioration of the pigments. This famous sermon is said to have taken place near Bevagna, on the opposite side of the Vale of Spoleto to Assisi, when the birds of the air flocked to hear St Francis. His homily on this occasion was more for the benefit of the human onlookers, for he emphasised that, just as God provides for the humble sparrow so He will look after the needs of the humble, so long as they are content with little.

Scene 16 illustrates the death of the Knight of Celano, whose last confession St Francis had just heard, miraculously anticipating that the man was about to die. In the next, an amusing scene, St Francis sits dumb before Pope Honorius III. Invited to preach to the Pope, Francis carefully prepared and memorised his sermon but his mind went blank at the critical moment. After praying to the Holy Spirit St Francis was inspired once again to eloquence.

The next scene depicts St Francis appearing miraculously to a conference of friars held at Arles, and the next shows the saint alone on Mount Alveriana (La Verna, in Tuscany) receiving the stigmata, the wounds of Christ, on his hands, side and feet. Biographers say that St Francis sought to conceal these wounds from his followers and that, though they gave him great pain, he nevertheless composed the Canticle to the Sun, a hymn of praise for God's creation, shortly afterwards – determined to be, as he taught his followers, always joyful even in the face of pain and adversity.

The next scene shows the death and apotheosis of the saint and a parallel scene in which Francis appears, after his death, to Friar Agostino and the Bishop of Assisi. Scene 22 deliberately draws further parallels between the lives of Christ and St Francis. Just as St Thomas doubted that Christ had truly risen until he touched his wounded body, so a certain incredulous knight called Girolamo is shown examining the body of St Francis to prove the truth of the stigmata.

In the following beautifully composed and expressive fresco, St Clare pays her last respects to St Francis as his funeral cortège pauses in front of San Damiano, the church that St Francis rebuilt (though not in the fanciful Gothic style depicted by Giotto) and gave to the Poor Clares as their mother convent.

This rich and crowded scene is the last attributed to Giotto. The next three are the work of pupils and the last two are credited to an anonymous 'St Cecilia Master', so called because it is believed that the same artist painted the *Life of St Cecilia* now hanging in the Uffizi in Florence.

The first of the three depicts Pope Gregory presiding over the canonisation ceremony for St Francis that took place on 16 July 1228. Next, the saint appears to the Pope in a vision. Finally, three miracles are illustrated: St Francis healing the wounds of Giovanni di Lerida; the dead woman restored to life long enough to make her final confession; and the liberation of Pietro di Alife, falsely accused of heresy, from imprisonment.

The town

Although the great fresco cycle in the Basilica di San Francesco ends with a series of miracles, one of the distinctive features of Assisi is that pilgrims come here to celebrate St Francis, not to seek supernatural intervention in their lives. In this respect Assisi is a very different sort of pilgrim town to, say, Cascia where the visitors flock to seek the help of St Rita (patron saint of parents, the infertile and all those in desperate situations!).

Assisi attracts large numbers of young people from all over the world – not necessarily even Christian – who recognise universal truths in the teaching of St Francis. They come to seek inspiration in the example he set and the values he espoused – humility, simplicity, love of the natural world and, above all, cheerfulness.

St Francis saw himself as the 'jongleur de Dieu', God's troubadour, and he taught his followers to be 'joyful and merry before the Lord'. Song played an important part in Franciscan worship. St Francis himself wrote celebratory hymns in the vernacular tongue, shrewdly adopting the rhythms and forms of popular contemporary ballads that had been introduced to Italy by Provençal troubadours – the equivalent, today, of hymns written in the style of pop songs (St Francis was, incidentally, the son of a Provençal mother and his name, Francesco, means 'little Frenchman'). That is why, as you wander round the town, you will quite commonly hear groups of young pilgrims break into spontaneous song (ignoring notices that command 'Silenzio' in the basilica). That is why, too, as you explore Assisi you will encounter smiling happy crowds, and this uniquely joyful atmosphere does much to compensate for the fact that much of the town centre is devoted to the sale of often tasteless souvenirs.

Via San Francesco to the Piazza del Comune

Via San Francesco has more to offer than majolica plates, embroidered blouses, wooden crucifixes and leather sandals. Looking up you will see many a handsome Renaissance façade above the shop windows, many with windows framed by the characteristic Umbrian arch with its pronounced inverted teardrop keystone at the apex.

At Nos 14–16, on the left, are the stumpy remains of a 13th-century defensive tower, to which the owners could retreat in troubled times, alongside a 15th-century façade with Renaissance torch-holders, terminating in animal-head finials. This palazzo was once the headquarters of the Guild of Masons and bears the Guild's insignia – a flower and a pair of compasses – as well as the date, 1477.

No.12, further up, is a fine 17th-century palazzo in classical style with aprons below the windows and an ornate balcony. This now serves as the Biblioteca Comunale (Municipal Library) where historians can study records relating to the history of Assisi and the Franciscans.

Opposite, at No.7, the Oratorio dei Pellegrine, or Pilgrim's Chapel, was converted to a hostel for pilgrims in 1431 and contains delicate frescoes by Antonio Mezzastris and Matteo di Gualdo. Nearby is the 14th-century Porticato del Monte Frumentario, the colonnade, now filled in, that once served as the town's grain market. Beyond, also on the right, is the Fonte Olivieri, a fountain and cistern dating to 1570 and bearing an inscription warning that anyone using the water for laundry will have their washing confiscated and be fined one scudo.

Via Seminario and Via Portica link Via San Francesco to the Piazzo del Comune. Just before the piazza, at Via Portica 2, there is an entrance to the Museo Romano. This is located in the crypt (all that survives) of the 11th-century church of San Nicolo. The crypt is used to display Roman coffins, architectural fragments and sculptures as well as some fine Etruscan funerary urns. A passage from the crypt leads beneath the Piazza del Comune to the subterranean remains of the Roman forum. The end wall supports the Temple of Minerva above, which once formed the focal point of the forum, and below the wall there are the remains of the stone dais, where the magistrates once had their seats, and a flight of steps leading to the Temple.

Emerging back into the daylight, the Temple of Minerva stands on the left-hand side of Piazza del Commune. Six time-worn but still elegant Corinthian columns that form the porch or pronaos pleased the German poet Goethe immensely. Journeying south to Rome he only had eyes for the antique and classical. He dismissed the basilica as a monstrous Babylonian pile; the temple, however, sent him into raptures, principally because it was the 'first complete monument of ancient days' that he had seen since arriving in Italy.

Unfortunately it is not as complete as Goethe suggests. The interior was rebuilt in 1634 as a church dedicated to San Filippo Neri. Even the official town guidebook candidly admits that 'the baroque ornamentations of the interior are a real disappointment'.

The civic buildings of Assisi are to the left of the temple. The Romanesque Torre del Comune (Municipal Tower) was begun in 1275 and remains as a reminder of the feuding that took place in the 13th and 14th centuries between the Guelph and Ghibelline factions. The towns of Umbria once bristled with such towers, built by wealthy aristocrats to guard their palazzi, but most were taken down or reduced in height as a result of ordinances designed to eliminate vendettas and private warfare.

Another reminder of those ancient conflicts is found in the battlements of the tower and the next-door Palazzo del Capitano del Popolo (Palace of the People's Captain). The tower has fishtail Ghibelline crenellations, the palazzo has square Guelph ones (the latter added in 1927, long after the cause and bitterness of these quarrels had been forgotten). A selection of 13th-century bricks and roof tiles is set into the tower wall alongside the portal, found when the palazzo, completed in 1282, was restored earlier this century.

Further up the square, on the opposite side, is the Palazzo dei Priori, the palace of the Priorate or governing council, still in use as the town hall. The palazzo is not one but four linked buildings, pierced by great tunnels, one of which is frescoed with colourful grotesque ornament. This haphazard group is not beautiful but the 14th-century façades are enlivened by massive wrought-iron lamps. The Pinacoteca Civica, on the first floor, contains a number of works by Umbrian painters.

The left-hand tunnel that passes beneath the palazzo descends to a small piazza dominated by the domed Chiesa Nuova. This was built in 1615 on the supposed site of the birthplace of St Francis. Just inside the door on the left is the cell in which St Francis was imprisoned for stealing his father's cloth and selling it to pay for the rebuilding of San Damiano.

More remains of the original house can be seen in the adjacent friary and you can stretch incredulity further by seeking out the saint's birthplace in Via di San Antonio, south of the church. Despite the fact that St Francis was born the son of a wealthy merchant, the 14th-century Latin inscription in the Oratorio di San Francesco Piccolino would have us believe that 'the light of the world, St Francis, was born in the stable of an ox and an ass'.

The Duomo

From the Piazza del Comune, take the leftmost street out of the square, Via San Rufino. This steep and narrow lane climbs to the upper part of the town and levels out at the Piazza San Rufino, in front of the cathedral.

Far fewer visitors ever reach this part of Assisi than crowd the lower town; indeed, few realise that the cathedral exists at all, tucked away as it is well away from the central square. Yet San Rufino has perhaps the most outstanding Romanesque façade in all of Umbria, a sculptural masterpiece, partnered by the massive and stately Romanesque campanile alongside.

San Rufino was the third cathedral to be built in Assisi. The first was Santa Maria Maggiore (see page 66). The second was founded on this site in 1029 by Bishop Ugone; the lower part of the campanile is all that survives. The third cathedral, the one we see now, was begun in 1140.

This site was chosen for the cathedral because, before the canonisation of St Francis, the town's principal saint was the early Christian martyr, San Rufino

The Romanesque Duomo in Assisi where St Francis, St Clare and the future Holy Roman Emperor, Frederick II, were all baptized

(d.238). His mausoleum was the site of a chapel as early as the 5th century which was enlarged in the 9th and then partly demolished to make way for Bishop Ugone's cathedral.

The crypt which held San Rufino's tomb can be entered through the door on the right side of the piazza (signposted 'Accesso al sotteraneo'). San Rufino himself was translated to a grave beneath the cathedral's main altar, but his 3rd-century marble sarcophagus, carved with reliefs illustrating the myth of Diana and Endymion, is displayed in the crypt. The faded frescoes of the

The splendid wheel window of the Duomo in Assisi is supported by comic caryatids and surrounded by symbols of the Evangelists

Evangelists on the walls are now dated to the 11th century and not, as previously thought, to the 3rd.

The principal attraction of the cathedral, however, is its marvellous façade. This is divided into three parts, both vertically and horizontally, and there is a pleasing symmetry to the whole composition rarely found on other façades of similar date.

The middle tier, horizontally, is separated from the lower one by a running arcade. With binoculars you can see that the arcade plinth and the corbels below are carved with lively representations of human, animal and bird heads; two oxen and two wolves stand guard where the arcade intersects the vertical pilasters.

Above, the central rose window is supported by three caryatids, comical figures straining under the supposed weight of the structure. Symbols of the Evangelists are carved at the corners of an imaginary square frame enclosing the whole window.

Below, the lunette of the central portal is carved with a charming scene, rustic in its execution but nonetheless expressive. In the centre is Christ seated in Majesty between the sun and the moon. San Rufino stands to the right, in vestments, while to the left the Virgin suckles the infant Christ.

It has been argued that this carving, which does not fit exactly into the allotted space, may be earlier than the rest of the façade, perhaps reused from Bishop Ugone's early 11th-century cathedral. Certainly the crudeness of the carving differs from the finer workmanship of the door mouldings, which are covered with vignettes of domestic and agricultural life, with angels, saints and troubadours, and with real and imaginary beasts (including a penguin and a crocodile) set amongst a running foliage frieze.

Two red marble lions crouch either side of the portal, the stone polished by countless generations of children who, despite the ferocity of the lions' features, have climbed upon their backs. One lion is gnawing a human head while the other is playing with its cub. No one has a satisfactory explanation for their symbolism. A suggestion that they represent the rejection of human sacrifice, distinguishing Christian from pagan religion, is scarcely convincing. They seem, rather, to belong to another age and culture altogether, like the lions and guardian spirits of some ancient Assyrian temple.

The two side lunettes are carved with paired doves (right) and lions (left) drinking from a vase – interpreted as symbolising the waters of life – and the crucifix above and imperial eagles below may represent the eternal and temporal powers.

Inevitably the interior of San Rufino will come as a disappointment, failing as it does to fulfil the promise of the exterior. At the back, though, to the right is an iron-bound marble font, originally from the first cathedral, which was used to baptise three future saints – Francis, Clare and Agnes – and the future Holy Roman Emperor, Frederick II, who was born prematurely outside the town (some say in the Marches town of Jesi) in 1194. Thus, within eight years of each other the two greatest men of their age were baptised in the same font: the emperor who spent much of his career trying to establish authority over the regions of Italy conquered by his grandfather, Frederick Barbarossa, and the saint who, according the emperor himself, did most to frustrate Frederick's ambitions by rekindling the spirit of his enemy, the Church.

The few other highlights of the cathedral are the carved wooden seats of the choir, dating to 1520, and the early 15th-century terracotta Pietà in the chapel to the left of the apse – called the Chapel of the Madonna of Tears because the statue is said to have wept on one occasion.

The Museo Capitolare, entered from the right of the apse, contains a fine triptych by Nicolo Alunno, one of the best of the early Umbrian painters, depicting the martyrdom of San Rufino. On leaving the cathedral look for the small door in the right-hand aisle near the exit; this leads down to the 1st-century BC Roman water storage cistern that now forms the foundation for the campanile.

The Rocca Maggiore

From the Duomo, anyone with the energy can visit, or revisit, the Rocca Maggiore (Great Fort) by climbing the steep stone staircase called Vicolo San Lorenzo. The castle has been described as 'well preserved' and 'much restored'. The latter is probably nearer the truth because the castle, once regarded as the foremost in Umbria, was much used as a quarry by local people seeking a readily available source of building materials, and was described as ruinous in the 18th century.

The first castle was built in 1174 at the order of Frederick Hohenstaufen, known to Italians as Barbarossa – Redbeard – who invaded Italy in 1155 to reassert the territorial claims of the Holy Roman Emperor against those of the Pope. Barbarossa's grandson, Frederick II, spent some time living in the castle under the care of Duke Conrad of Urslingen but in 1198 the people of Assisi destroyed the castle in an uprising against the Duke's tyrannical rule. The present castle therefore dates to the rebuilding, this time under papal control, of 1367, with enlargements and modifications carried out up to 1535.

The principal reason for making the effort to visit the fort is the panoramic view to be had from the tall central tower that served as the living quarters. Even if the summer haze obscures the Vale of Spoleto, the sight of the orange-brown rooftops of Assisi, the town's churches and campanile laid out below is sufficient reward.

The remaining sights of Assisi lie back in the lower town.

Santa Chiara

Most of the narrow lanes that lead south from the Piazza San Rufino eventually reach the Piazza Santa Chiara and its basilica, the burial place of St Clare, founder of the Poor Clares.

Although less ornate than the cathedral or the Basilica di San Francesco, the exterior of Santa Chiara is impressive enough just because of its great bulk, anchored to the ground by huge flying buttresses like some great pink and white wingless insect. The buttresses were added in the late 14th century to prevent the whole structure from collapsing.

In plan the basilica is a deliberate copy of the upper church of the Basilica di San Francesco. The interior was once as gorgeously frescoed as that church with scenes from the life of Santa Chiara. Sadly, the frescoes were covered with whitewash in the 17th century to deter visitors who were disturbing the contemplative life of the nuns. Some were uncovered again in the 1920s.

The basilica was begun in 1257 and is built alongside the little 12th-century church of San Giorgio. This was the church in which St Clare first set eyes on St Francis when, at the age of eighteen, she went to hear him preach a series of Lenten sermons.

A year later, St Clare sought out St Francis, who was living with a small community of followers, at the Porziuncola, a small church now contained

The Rocca Maggiore in Assisi, built by Frederick Barbarossa

within the huge domed basilica of Santa Maria degli Angeli which you can see in the valley below Assisi from the terrace in front of Santa Chiara.

In an episode that parallels St Francis's renunciation of worldly wealth, she stripped off her clothes, put on a sackcloth tunic and knelt before St Francis asking him to shear off her fine long hair. Again, as with St Francis, Clare's family tried to bring her to her senses, but she persuaded her 15-year-old sister, Agnes, and later her mother to give up everything and join her.

Eventually St Francis appointed Clare as the superior of a new order of Franciscan nuns, the Poor Clares, with San Damiano as its headquarters. Clare was fanatical in her rigorous pursuit of poverty and privation. The first rule that she drafted forbade members of the order to wear stockings or footwear. Her followers were to sleep on the hard ground, fast perpetually and never to speak except in prayer or to beg alms on behalf of the Franciscans.

This rule, considered too harsh, was modified by successive popes so that the Poor Clares evolved into a contemplative, rather than an active, order. St Clare herself scarcely left the confines of San Damiano in the forty years during which she served as head of the order, and suffered almost continuous ill health.

One Christmas Eve, ill and unable to attend the Christmas service, St Clare experienced a vision in which she saw the crib and the congregation singing in a church. For this reason, and of all the saints who have experienced visions, St Clare was singled out for a dubious and scarcely appropriate honour: in 1938, Pope Pius XII declared her the patron saint of television.

St Clare died in 1253 and was buried in San Damiano. Two years later she was canonised and two years after that the foundations of the new basilica were laid. In 1260 St Clare's body was translated to the crypt of the finished basilica and the Poor Clares moved from San Damiano to their new convent alongside their founder's shrine.

The speed with which the basilica was built accounts for its relative plainness and the later subsidence. The beauty of the exterior derives from the decorative bands of alternating rose and white limestone, and the delicate rose window that forms the principal ornament of the west front.

The exterior, and the tall companile that rises behind, are still essentially Romanesque in style, but the great aisle-less groin-vaulted nave is Gothic.

The best of the surviving frescoes are found in the transepts. On the end wall on the left (north) transept there is a touching Nativity scene painted in the 14th century and a mid 13th-century Virgin and Child. The latter, though repainted in the 1920s, is still a pure and powerful work in the Byzantine style.

On the opposite wall, in the south transept, there is a complete panel painted in a similar style, showing St Clare with highly stylised facial features and drapery. The central figure is surrounded by eight small scenes depicting the major events in her life. The scenes read from the left, starting at the bottom, as follows:

1. In the Palm Sunday service, held in the cathedral of San Rufino, the Bishop

of Assisi singles out the shy and retiring Clare to receive a palm, knowing that she is destined for great things.

2. Clare escapes from her family home and seeks out St Francis at San Damiano.
3. Clare, dressed in a rough habit, has her hair shorn by St Francis.
4. Clare's father tries to force her to return home.
5. Two scenes: in the upper portion of the picture, St Clare welcomes her sister, St Agnes, to the convent of San Damiano; below, their father tries to seize Agnes but miraculously her body becomes too heavy to lift and his hand, about to strike Agnes, is suddenly paralysed.
6. St Clare blesses bread in the refectory at San Damiano and each piece is miraculously marked with a cross.
7. St Clare, on her deathbed, has a vision of the heavenly city filled with crowned virgins.
8. Pope Innocent IV officiates at the funeral of St Clare.

Near to this fresco is a door that leads to the original church of San Giorgio, now subdivided into two chapels. The Cappella del Sacramento, the Chapel of the Blessed Sacrament, contains fresco scenes from the life of Christ and a fine Virgin enthroned with St Clare, St Francis, John the Baptist and the Archangel Michael, attributed to a follower of Giotto.

Next door, in the Cappella del Crocifisso, you will find the 12th-century painted crucifix which, according to Franciscan legend, spoke to St Francis in the ruined church of San Damiano, commanding him to rebuild the church. The Poor Clares brought the crucifix with them when they relocated to Santa Chiara, along with the rough woollen habit of St Clare and the locks of hair which St Clare cut from her head; these relics are displayed in a case in the same chapel.

The remains of St Clare herself are displayed in the crypt beneath the high altar, a rather ugly neo-classical edifice which, for all that the walls are lined with rare marbles, does little to inspire a sense of reverence. Clare's body was rediscovered in 1850 and, as you would expect of a saint, her body was found to be perfectly preserved when her coffin was opened. She did not long survive exposure to the open air and deteriorated rapidly until human hands intervened to produce the saintly sleeping figure that lies in the crypt today.

Santa Maria Maggiore

From Santa Chiara it is well worth walking down the Via Santa Agnese to the Piazza Vescovado and the little church of Santa Maria Maggiore. This is a relatively plain building, and not much visited, so you can recollect in tranquillity the important part it played in the early history of Assisi.

The church stands on the foundations of a Roman temple to Janus. Parts of the crypt date to the 4th century when an early Christian church was first built here reusing Roman masonry. It later served as Assisi's cathedral until 1029 when Bishop Ugone began to build San Rufino. The present structure dates from 1163. The date is carved on one of the spokes of the wheel window in the west façade along with the name of the architect – Giovanni (da Gubbio) – the same man who, seven years later, went on to design the present cathedral.

In the quiet of this church it is possible to picture the events that occurred here when, at the end of the 12th century, St Francis, and later Frederick II were baptised, and when, at the beginning of the 13th, in the next-door Vescovado, the Bishop's Palace, St Francis stripped off his clothes, renounced all possessions and wandered off into the Umbrian countryside to spark a revolution in the history of Christianity.

The environs of Assisi

In Assisi the countryside that St Francis loved seems ever present. No other town in Umbria is so colourful with flowers. Lacking gardens of any size, the people of Assisi show great ingenuity in finding space in which to grow their plants. Sunflowers and tomatoes, grapevines and roses, oleanders and bright red pelargoniums spill out of tubs and pots that almost block the narrow streets, on staircases and window sills, and suspended on iron hoops cemented to the rose-pink walls of the medieval houses.

Swallows wheel and dive over the rooftops and bees and butterflies come into the town to feed. Whenever you look up to the highest point of the town, you see the wild, deep green slopes of Mount Subasio, clothed in holm oak and acacia. When you step out through the Porta Nuova, at the eastern end of the town, it is like stepping from a tamed garden into a slightly wilder countryside. It is true that you first have to negotiate the road that encircles Assisi, the Viale Vittorio Emanuele II, but once over this busy highway, you reach the fields.

San Damiano

The steep pedestrian road that leads to San Damiano, just over half a mile (1km) away, passes through tranquil olive groves where ancient and gnarled trees rise from a carpet of wildflowers and tall dark cypresses signal the direction to the little sanctuary.

Like many Franciscan establishments, San Damiano is a humble building of rough unadorned stone; it could be mistaken for a farmhouse but for the simple arcade in front of the church and the cloisters, added in the 16th century.

Inside the church, on the right, 14th-century frescoes recall the decisive incident in the life of St Francis when Christ spoke to him from the cross saying 'Vade, Francisce, et repera domum meum' (Go, Francis, and repair my house). Another scene shows St Francis offering money for the restoration of San Damiano and then being pursued by his angry father. These scenes surround a niche which was once a small window; when the priest in charge of San Damiano refused to accept the money offered to him, St Francis left it on this window sill.

The chapel on the right contains a remarkable crucifix; not the one that spoke to St Francis, which is now in Santa Chiara, but an outstandingly lifelike work by Friar Innocenzo di Palermo, carved in 1637. This evidently gifted artist, however, is not given full credit: it is said that Innocenzo carved the body and left the work unfinished overnight. When he returned the next day he found the head miraculously completed. Moreover, the head of Christ has three different expressions – anguish, death and tranquillity – depending on whether you view it from the left, right or centre.

From the church you pass into the Choir of St Clare, a bare room furnished with a lectern and benches of rough-hewn wooden planks in which Clare and her companions would meet at intervals during the day and night for prayer. The same chapel contains a recess, the cell in which St Francis is said to have hidden for a month from his angry father.

Narrow staircases and tiny doorways force you to stoop as you climb to the little open-air terrace where St Clare spent much of her life, and the dormitory in which she died, the spot usually marked by a small vase of white flowers.

The exit from the dormitory leads to the beautiful cloister filled with pots of lilies, pelargoniums and oleanders, where lizards bask in the sunshine, scurrying away up to the rooftops if disturbed. More flowers fill the fantasy landscape which forms the background to a 1507 fresco by Eusebio di San Giorgio showing St Francis receiving the stigmata.

Finally, a door leads off the cloister to the refectory of the Poor Clares, a low room with smoke-darkened vaults and its original rough tables and benches. Again the place habitually occupied by St Clare is usually marked by flowers. A fresco by Doni, of the Crucifixion, intrudes on the moving simplicity of this room. Another wall is marked with the word 'Silentium'. For once, everyone who visits this humble spot obeys, for few other places associated with St Francis and St Clare so well evoke the life of utmost poverty that they chose, in rejection of the richness and power of the Church of their time.

Linger and enjoy the tranquillity of San Damiano for a while, for the next point on the itinerary is entirely different.

The Basilica of Santa Maria degli Angeli

It is impossible to spend time in Assisi without catching sight of the huge dome of the Basilica of Santa Maria degli Angeli in the plain below the town. The monumental basilica is nearly 6km south of Assisi and best reached by car to avoid the long hot climb back to the town.

Few commentators have much to say in favour of the basilica itself. It was begun in 1569 but reconstructed after an earthquake in 1832 and remodelled in 1926. Its great bulk seems more fitting for the monument of some emperor or military giant than that of the humblest of saints.

Do not, however, let the exterior deter you from visiting, nor the souvenir stalls that ring the walls, for inside, beneath the dome of the vast echoing nave, is a simple rustic village chapel preserved in its entirety.

The chapel is known as the Porziuncola, a term that means a small portion – perhaps referring to the small parcel of land, a clearing in the woods, on which the chapel was built. It is said that the chapel was founded in the 3rd or 4th century by pilgrims returning from the Holy Land, to hold a fragment of the Virgin's tomb. In the 6th century St Benedict, Umbria's other great saint and founder of Western monasticism, visited this spot and established a small monastic cell.

By the early 13th century the Porziuncola was roofless and the Benedictines agreed to give it to St Francis as a base for his newly established order. St Francis, true to the principle of absolute poverty, preferred to rent rather than own it, and agreed to give the Benedictines one basket of fish, caught in the nearby River Tescio, as an annual payment; this symbolic rent continues to be paid.

It is said that St Francis himself built the vault that now covers the chapel and around it he established a small community of friars who lived in wattle and daub huts in the surrounding woods. It was here that St Clare came to seek out St Francis and to take the habit of a nun, and here that the Franciscans held their first ever convocation in 1219, attended by over 5,000 friars from all over Europe – the so-called Chapter of the Stuoie (mats) after the woven straw mattresses on which the delegates slept. It was here, too, that St Francis died in 1226, having refused the offer of a room in the Bishop of Assisi's palace. Today it is hard to reconstruct, mentally, the appearance of the woodland environment in which all these momentous events took place, around the simple stone chapel, so much does the gaudiness of the surrounding basilica intrude on the senses. Inside the little chapel, however, something of the original Franciscan spirit is still present in the austere, blackened walls, almost totally devoid of distracting ornament.

The one fresco, above the altar, was executed by Viterbo in 1393. It shows the *Annunciation* and *Christ in Majesty* with four scenes from the life of St Francis – including the granting of an indulgence, by Pope Honorius III in 1216, to all those who visit the church on 1 or 2 August; days on which, to the present time, large numbers of pilgrims visit the church to receive the 'Pardon of St Francis'.

Beyond the chapel, in the sanctuary to the right, another structure, called the Cappella del Transito, marks the site of the infirmary and the spot on which St Francis died. Inside, the frescoes of 1516 by Giovanni di Pietro (also known as Lo Spagna) depict Franciscan saints and there is a very lifelike and ascetic figure of St Francis in white-glazed terracotta above the altar, the work of Andrea della Robbia.

More of della Robbia's work can be seen in the crypt beneath the choir which is formed, in part, from masonry representing the foundations of one of the earliest monastic buildings to be erected on the site in the 13th century. Andrea della Robbia's bas reliefs over the main altar are regarded as being among this Renaissance artist's finest work; they depict St Francis receiving the stigmata, the Coronation of the Virgin, St Jerome, the Annunciation, the Nativity and the Adoration of the Magi.

The right transept leads to the sacristy, lined with 17th-century inlaid wood cupboards, and then on to a series of rooms where tourist kitsch begins, progressively, to dominate – you are greeted, for example, by a pair of white doves who have been trained to sit on the hands of a mawkish statue of St Francis and coo at passers by.

The corridor with the doves leads past the Rosery, a tiny triangular garden tucked beneath the basilica walls and planted with roses. These are no ordinary roses, as a nearby plaque explains in eloquent terms. They descend from the roses into which St Francis threw himself naked one winter's night while wrestling with the devil's temptations.

St Francis intended to castigate himself but, instead, 'white and red roses, wonderfully perfumed, sprang up and blossomed on all sides and a multitude of angels descended and ranged themselves around the church.' Moreover, the thorns dropped from the rose stems and they remain thornless to this day, their leaves streaked with markings the colour of blood.

In the Cappella delle Rose, alongside, standing on the site of St Francis's hut, beautifully fresh frescoes, executed by Tiberio di Assisi in 1518, depict this delightful story and other events in the life of the saint.

After these charming paintings it is difficult to find any merit in the modern tableaux illustrating religious subjects, complete with moving mannequins, that have been mounted in the rooms beyond.

The museum off the cloisters does, however, contain some good works of art: notably a crucifix by Pisano, painted in 1236 and contemporary with the cross which spoke to St Francis in the church of San Damiano; a picture of St Francis between two angels, painted by the anonymous Maestro di San Francesco on boards from the bed on which St Francis is said to have died (hagiographers say he died on the bare earth); and another painted on boards from the saint's coffin. The latter was once attributed to Cimabue because it is so like that artist's famous 'portrait from life' in the Basilica di San Francesco, but it is now thought to be a copy of Cimabue's portrait by one of his pupils.

Eremo delle Carceri

The final destination on our tour of Franciscan places around Assisi is the idyllic Eremo delle Carceri, the hermitage set in the woods half way up Monte Subasio. To reach the hermitage you have to return to Assisi and leave by the Porta Cappuccini, east of the town, and take the uphill road that leads past the town's campsite. From here it is 5km to the hermitage up a steep twisting road. If you choose to walk you will be rewarded by the rich flora that grows on the verges and on the exposed rock faces, and by wide-ranging views. On the other hand you will rarely have the road to yourself, especially in summer when cars and coaches, heading for the hermitage, pay scant respect to pedestrians.

Since the hermitage is open from 6.30 to 17.30, the best time to visit is

The Eremo delle Carceri, set among evergreen oaks on the slopes of Monte Subasio, was St Francis's favourite retreat

first thing in the morning, at lunch time or, best of all, at the end of the day when the countryside is illuminated by the glow of the western sun and there are few other visitors.

The hermitage has all the charm of the simplest of Franciscan retreats. The order rarely built grandiose monasteries and favoured simple structures, sometimes no more than a hillside cave, where nothing would distract the friars from prayer and contemplation. The hermitage is just such a place.

The name Eremo delle Carceri is misleadingly translated as Hermitage of the Prisons. Carceri may mean prisons in modern Italian but in medieval times the term simply denoted a remote place, an enclosure or stockade away from the town. Even today, despite the number of visitors, the hermitage does still have the feeling of remoteness, isolated as it is in a sea of evergreen holm oak.

Even so, the hermitage is more substantial now than it was in the 13th century when St Francis first came here as a young man, his plans to become a crusader frustrated by illness, to try and work out the future direction of his life. He returned at frequent intervals, living in a cave and sleeping on a stone ledge with a log for a pillow, and always called this spot his favourite retreat.

That cave, the Grotta di San Francesco, survives at the core of the modern complex, reached through a tiny narrow passageway and staircase off the diminutive chapel of Santa Maria. The chapel itself, and the cloister, were added in the early 15th century and the remainder of the buildings are of more recent date.

At the southern end of the hermitage a path leads to a stone bridge which crosses a precipitous ravine. This is the site of several miracles attributed to St Francis. On one occasion he cast a devil into a crevice in the rocks by the power of prayer alone.

On another he commanded the stream that once gushed down the mountainside to dry up; the noise of the torrent was distracting the friars in their prayers (a most uncharacteristic act, one might think, from a man who praised the waters of the earth, 'so useful and humble, so precious and pure', in his *Canticle to the Sun* – but then, hagiographers care nothing for consistency). The stream continues to be dry; on the rare occasions when water does flow, the people of Assisi get worried, for this is regarded as an inauspicious event, heralding some great calamity.

By the side of the bridge, hanging over the brink of the ravine, is a broken and weather-tossed holm oak, anchored by iron braces and collars and so ancient that it struggles to bear any leaves; a pitiful sight, but this tree has survived six centuries since the time when the birds used to gather in its branches to listen to St Francis preaching.

From this spot several pathways penetrate the dense woodland that surrounds the hermitage, and, following them, you will glimpse mountainside caves once occupied by St Francis and his followers. Few visitors step beyond the confines of the hermitage and if you come this far you will find many a tranquil spot for reflecting on the gentle beauty of the unspoiled Umbrian countryside.

Practical Information

Tourist information office

Piazza del Comune 12 (tel. 075 812534)

Where to stay

There is plenty of accommodation in Assisi and nearby, but you should book well in advance if you intend to visit during July and August, or during the festival of Calendimaggio at the beginning of May.

Hotel Subasio, Via Frate Elia 2 (tel. 075-812 206): Right next to the Basilica di San Francesco, with wonderful views from many rooms. Expensive, as you would expect from a hotel that has played host to royalty and film stars, including Charlie Chaplin.

Hotel Fontebella, Via Fontebella 25 (tel. 075-812 883): Midway between the basilica and the main square, this converted 17th-century palazzo is the main rival to the Subasio in the luxury class. Like the Subasio, the Fontebella has a garage for guests, a considerable advantage since parking within Assisi is always problematical.

Hotel Umbra, Via degli Archi 6 (tel. 075-812 240): Just off the main square, a hotel of character with one of Assisi's best restaurants (hotel closed 10 Jan –15 March).

Ideale per Turisti, Piazza Matteotti 1 (tel. 075-813 570): Small (9 rooms), modern, central and inexpensive with views over the Parco del Pincio.

Agriturismo (tel. 075-812 659), is the agency to contact for a list of farms in the Assisi area offering bed, breakfast and dinner or self-catering accommodation.

Camping (tel. 075-813 636) and **Youth Hostel** (tel. 075-812 317): Both on the same site at Fontemaggio, just under half a mile east of Assisi and set in an attractive olive grove.

Where to eat

Buca di San Francesco, Via Brizi 1 (tel. 075-812 204): Expensive but regarded as the best in Assisi for regional cuisine and fine wines. Choose whether to dine in the atmospheric medieval cellars or the well-planted garden (closed Mon and 7 Jan–28 Feb).

Umbra, Via degli Archi 6 (tel. 075-812 240): The restaurant of the hotel of the same name, family-run and specialising in dishes that draw on the finest local products (closed Tues and 15 Nov–15 Dec).

La Fortezza, Vicolo della Fortezza 2B (tel. 075-812 418): Another fine, and marginally cheaper, restaurant renowned for truffle dishes and the house speciality, wild rabbit in asparagus sauce (closed Thurs).

Pizzeria il Pozzo Romano, Via Sant' Agnese: Cheap, and popular with young visitors, especially since it stays open late.

6. PERUGIA

The contrast between Perugia and Assisi could not be greater. From the intimacy and quiet of Assisi's immaculately clean and flower-filled streets you travel by congested highways to the bustling capital of Umbria, a mere 32km by road but a world away in character and atmosphere.

Getting into the city at all is a battle since cars are virtually excluded from the city centre and parking spaces around the periphery fill well before 9am. The best place to try is along the Corso Cavour, near the church of San Pietro, or the car park in Piazza di Partigiani, next to the bus station, which is linked to the city centre by an escalator (scala mobile).

Wherever you park, head first for the wide avenue, the Corso Vannucci, that forms the main street of Perugia. Free from traffic, this is the best place in Umbria for people watching and for tuning into the rhythms of the city. Perugia's lively atmosphere is created by the large number of students who come here to study at the ancient University and the Academy of Fine Arts, their numbers swelled by foreign students studying at the University for Foreigners and lending their own contribution to the cosmopolitanism of the city. They ensure that the nightlife of Perugia is never dull, especially during July's Umbria Jazz Festival.

By day, too, the streets are filled with milling crowds of students, whiling away the time between lectures, absorbed in the rituals of coquetry and flirtation, which Italian girls have refined to an art, and showing off their expensive designer accessories.

Those who can afford to do so watch all this from the comfort of one of the Corso Vannucci's numerous pavement cafés. Students and impecunious travellers group together on the steps in front of the Duomo, forming a crowd that is at once the audience to the drama of the street life below, and itself part of the action.

The Duomo

The Duomo sits broadside on to the Piazza IV Novembre (locals simply call it the Piazza Grande), which closes off the northern end of the Corso Vannucci. Begun in 1345, the Duomo looks as if the masons simply downed tools one day and walked off, leaving the building half-finished. The stretch of marble

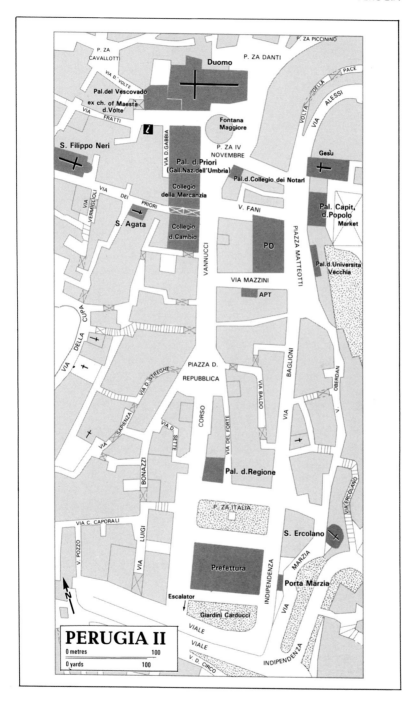

P. ZA PICCININO
P. ZA CAVALLOTTI
VIA D. VOLTE
Duomo
P. ZA DANTI
VOLTA DELLA PACE
VIA ALESSI
Pal.del Vescovado
ex ch. of Maestà
d.Volte
VIA FRATTI
Fontana
Maggiore
ℹ
VIA D.GABBIA
S. Filippo Neri
P. ZA IV
NOVEMBRE
Gesù
Pal. d.Priori
(Gall.Naz.dell'Umbria)
Pal.d.Collegio dei Notari
VIA DEI
PRIORI
Collegio
della Mercanzia
V. FANI
Pal. Capit.
d.Popolo
Market
VIA VERMIGLIOLI
S. Agata
Collegio
d.Cambio
VANNUCCI
PO
PIAZZA MATTEOTTI
Pal.d.Universita
Vecchia
VIA MAZZINI
APT
VIA DELLA CUPA
VIA D.STRECHE
PIAZZA D.
REPUBBLICA
BAGLIONI
OBERDAN
VIA SAPIENZA
VIA D. SETTE
CORSO
VIA BALDO
VIA DEL FORTE
VIA
Pal. d.Regione
BONAZZI
VIA C. CAPORALI
P. ZA ITALIA
VIA ERCOLANO
VIA LUIGI
V. POZZO
S. Ercolano
MARZIA
Prefettura
INDIPENDENZA
Porta Marzia
VIA
N
Escalator
Giardini Carducci
VIALE
INDIPENDENZA
PERUGIA II
VIALE
0 metres   100
V. D. CIRCO
0 yards   100

cladding on the southern flank, pierced by quatrefoils, indicates the intended final appearance of the cathedral exterior. The marble was taken as booty from the cathedral at Arezzo in 1335 but, following another battle shortly afterwards, the Perugians were forced to give most of it back, leaving their own cathedral with its present rough and ready appearance.

By contrast the four-arched Loggia di Braccio, to the left of the cathedral steps, is an elegant and early example of the revival of classical architecture that characterises the Renaissance; it was built in 1423.

To the left of the cathedral entrance is a bronze statue of Pope Julius III made by Vincenzo Danti in 1553 to commemorate the restitution of Papal authority over the city after centuries of bloody feuding between the leading families.

To the right is an elegant, but incomplete, outdoor pulpit dating to the first quarter of the 15th century. From here the fundamentalist Franciscan, Bernardino of Siena, preached to Perugians in 1425 and 1427. He urged them to abandon their materialistic and ungodly ways, and to burn their fine clothes, wigs, books and mirrors, much as the notorious Savonarola was to do in Florence when he instituted the 'Bonfires of Vanity' in the 1490s, some 60 years later.

The cathedral suffered damage in the earthquake of 1983 and the first thing you notice, on stepping inside the spacious and uncluttered nave, is that several of the simulated marble columns at the rear now lean in an alarming manner.

The Cappella del Sant' Anello (Chapel of the Holy Ring; first on the left as you face the high altar) is used to house a gold reliquary. This in turn contains fifteen further containers, fitted one within the other like a nest of Russian dolls, each with a unique lock. The keys are held by fifteen different citizens of Perugia and they come together once a year to reveal the contents of the innermost box: a piece of the Virgin's wedding ring, stolen by a Perugian woman from Chiusi cathedral in 1473. Fear of reprisals by Chiusans accounts for the elaborate security. A painting by Perugino, of the *Betrothal of the Virgin*, which once hung in this chapel was itself stolen by Napoleon and now hangs in the museum at Caen.

Further down on the left, the Chapel of the Banner contains a colourful and lively painting by Berto di Giovanni, dated to 1526, showing *Christ in Majesty* looking down on the people of Perugia. In the middle ground is a detailed view of the city as it looked in the early 16th century. This gonfalone, or banner, was made to be carried in religious processions called Misericordia, usually held when the city was in the grip of plague or warfare and intended to invoke God's mercy and aid.

On the opposite side of the nave, the chapel at the rear contains an animated and realistic *Deposition* by Federico Barocchio (1569), said to have been painted when the artist was high on some kind of poison fed to him by a jealous rival artist. The painting was much admired by Rubens and provided the inspiration for his own masterpiece, the *Descent from the Cross* in Antwerp cathedral.

On the third pillar down from here an altar stands in front of a sweet painting of the Virgin by Giannicola di Paolo (the unfortunate crown was added more recently). The rest of the pillar is covered in heart-shaped silver tokens, offerings from grateful mothers who venerate this image and pray to it for help in childbirth.

The best of the cathedral's surviving frescoes are in the sacristy, off the chancel to the right. They depict the life of St Lawrence, to whom the cathedral is dedicated, and Old Testament scenes, dating from around 1578 and executed by Pandolfi da Pesaro. Behind lies a peaceful cloister and the cathedral museum, whose highlights include Signorelli's *Madonna and Saints* and some beautiful early illuminated manuscripts dating from the 6th to the 13th centuries.

The Fontana Maggiore

Emerging from the cathedral you descend to the Fontana Maggiore, the Great Fountain, which stands in the middle of the square, an outstanding monument to that most humble and yet essential of commodities, water.

The fountain consists of two polygonal basins, one on top of the other, surmounted by a bronze bowl and three female figures. The whole composition dates to 1277 when Friar Bevignate, an expert on hydraulics, took charge of a publicly funded scheme to bring water into the heart of Perugia. He designed a system of aqueducts and underground pipes to bring the water from Monte Pacciano, a distance of nearly 3km.

Such an important enterprise demanded that the fountain to be built at the end of this system should be decorated by the leading sculptors of the day, Nicolo Pisano and his son Giovanni. The work of these two artists is remarkable. In contrast to the formalistic Gothic style of the time they developed a remarkably realistic style that foreshadows the achievements of Renaissance sculptors.

The lower basin has twenty-five sides, each subdivided into two panels. Beginning on the south side, furthest away from the cathedral, they illustrate: the Labours of the Months, each with the appropriate zodiacal sign; a griffin and a lion, symbolising Perugia and the Guelph party; the Liberal Arts; two eagles and the signature of Giovanni Pisano; Adam and Eve and their expulsion from the Garden of Eden; Samson and the Lion and Samson and Delilah; a man beating lion cubs, and David and Goliath; Romulus and Remus and the twins being suckled by a wolf watched over by a Vestal Virgin; and scenes from two of Aesop's Fables – the Wolf and the Crane and the Wolf and the Lamb.

This eclectic mixture of Christian and pagan, secular and religious, fabulous and mythical subjects is remarkable in itself as an insight into the medieval imagination, and the upper basin is equally diverse in its range of subject matter. Here, twenty-four statues ornament the angles, representing personifications of Perugia (a woman holding a cornucopia), of nearby Lake Trasimeno

Perugia's main square, the Piazza IV Novembre, with the elegant Fontana Maggiore and the Palazzo dei Priori

(a woman holding a fish), of Euliste, the mythical founder of Perugia, of saints, monks, evangelists and Old Testament prophets and even of the Governor of Perugia, Herman of Sassoferato, holding a sceptre.

On top of all this, the three bronze watercarriers, with interlinked arms, cast by Giovanni Pisano, have been variously interpreted as representing the Three Graces or the Three Theological Virtues.

The Palazzo dei Priori

When the Pisani were working on their beautiful fountain, the scene in the main square looked very different to what we see today. The site opposite the Duomo was occupied by a miscellaneous group of buildings, including the church of San Severo, all of which were swept away around 1300 to make way for the Palazzo dei Priori.

The same talented friar, Fra Bevignate, who designed the water works is credited with the design of the palace. The building was not, however, solely the work of any one architect or period. It was constructed over three centuries, only taking on its final appearance in the late 16th century.

Despite that, the palace exterior is a unified architectural whole, and Perugians, with justice, call it the most beautiful public building in Italy. Unity is provided by the two tiers of 14th-century windows that pierce the rugged walls of pink and white stone, quarried at Bettona. The windows of the lower tier have Gothic lancets contained within rectangular frames, while those above are surmounted by a triangular apex.

The regularity is broken on the south side by an elegant fan staircase. This was added in 1902, though its foot-worn stone steps seem much older and, as an inspired piece of design, the staircase lends grace to an otherwise rather masculine building.

The steps lead to the entrance of the Sala dei Notari, the Notaries' Room, originally a public meeting room but reused by city lawyers as a council chamber from 1583. Stone brackets above the portal support a brass griffin, the symbol of Perugia, cast in 1274, and a Guelph lion. The iron chains hanging from the brackets are said to have been taken in 1358 as war trophies from the gates of the defeated city of Siena, though it is likely that they once supported some more substantial booty, long since disappeared.

Inside, the Sala dei Notari (open 9.00–13.00, 15.00–18.00) is gorgeously frescoed with the coats of arms of the highest ranking citizens of Perugia and the effect, when the morning sun pours in through the windows, is of a mass of rich deep reds and blues. Scenes from fable and the Old Testament are painted in the spandrels of the eight massive arches that sail over the hall. They are attributed to various local 15th-century artists and were well restored in 1860. Below, the solid dais and ranks of wooden benches lining the walls give an idea of the arrangement of a Renaissance-period council chamber.

Collegio della Mercanzia and Collegio del Cambio

The long main façade of the palace, fronting on to Corso Vannucci, has two side doors before the principal entrance. One door leads to the little Sala del Collegio della Mercanzia (Room of the Merchant's Guild; open Tues–Sat 9.00–12.30, 15.00–18.00; Sun 9.00–12.30; closed Mon). The room is lined from floor to ceiling with 15th-century panelling of poplar and walnut, forming repeated patterns of quatrefoils within square frames.

The other door leads to the Collegio del Cambio, the Exchange Guild, one of Perugia's unmissable sights (open Tues–Sat 9.00–12.30, 14.30–17.30; Sun 9.00–12.30; closed Mon March–Sept; Tues–Sun 8.00–14.00; closed Mon Nov–Feb). The Exchange (also known as the Bankers' or Money Changers') Guild took over the use of this room in 1452. In 1496 the members of the Guild commissioned the local artist Pietro Vannucci – known to posterity as Perugino – to paint the walls. The result is regarded as his masterpiece, and one of the great achievements of the Italian Renaissance.

These frescoes bring together two distinct but related strands in the cultural development of the period. Following precedents set by Florentine sculptors and painters, the artists of the 15th century were striving towards a greater realism in their work. They rejected Gothic formality and, inspired by antique Greek and Roman sculpture, were learning to represent the human body with great expressive force and to compose dramatic scenes set in apparently three-dimensional space.

Concurrently, humanist writers and thinkers were rediscovering the lost literature of the Greeks and Romans. The works of Cicero were discovered in a remote Eastern monastery by the Florentine explorer, Poggio Bracciolini. The *Dialogues of Plato*, written in a language that had all but been forgotten until Cosimo de' Medici brought Manuel Chrysolarses to Florence to teach ancient Greek, were causing great excitement, and posing the challenging question of how these obviously important pagan teachings could be reconciled with Christian doctrine.

The frescoes of the Collegio del Cambio reveal part of the answer. The scheme for the frescoes was drawn up by the humanist scholar, Francesco Matoranzio. His theme is that parallels can be traced between the Bible and pagan philosophies, that the classical Greek and Roman writers were, in many senses, proto-Christian for, even if they believed in a multitude of gods, their ethical and moral principles were at one with Christianity.

Hence the frescoes blend pagan and Christian symbols. On the left-hand wall we find the allegorical figures of Prudence and Justice above historical figures whose life and works have exemplified those qualities, including Socrates and the Emperor Trajan; then Strength and Temperance exemplified by Pericles and Leonidas, amongst others.

Between the two Perugino painted his own self-portrait with unabashed realism; he frowns from beneath his red cap, a plump-featured man with a double chin and heavy black eyebrows. Commentators have found his appearance at odds with their expectations – as if the artist whose trademark is limpid, lyrical landscapes should himself possess correspondingly delicate features.

One of those beautiful landscapes, suffused with the dawn sunlight, forms the background to the Nativity scene on the end wall. Perugino was acknowledged, even in his own time, as a master of three-dimensional perspective, and the Nativity demonstrates fully that particular gift. We glimpse the landscape of wooded hills and winding streams through a series of arches, under which the shepherds kneel. The arches are supported on classical columns – another reference to the continuity which humanists sought between the ancient world and their own Christian civilisation.

That theme continues on the next wall, where God in Majesty is surrounded both by Old Testament prophets and by the Sybils who are supposed to have prophesied the birth of Christ to the Emperor Augustus, while pagan divinities crowd the vaulted ceiling.

Two smaller rooms lead off this one; the Chapel of St John the Baptist, with frescoes by Perugino's pupil, Giannicola di Paolo, executed 1513–28, and a meeting room with benches carved by Giampietro Zuccari, 1615–21.

The main doorway of the Palazzo dei Priori is surrounded by a richly carved portal, covered in trails of foliage that provide the frame for a series of allegorical scenes. The meaning of many can now only be guessed at, but the little scenes on the outermost columns, rising from the backs of two marble lions, represent Avarice, Greed and Humility (left) and Generosity, Fertility and Pride (right).

Two Perugian griffins on the brackets above are mauling calves, the symbol of the town's Guild of Butchers, who paid for the construction of the portal.

The palace is still used as the headquarters of the local authority that governs the Commune of Perugia, but the upper floors, reached by means of a lift house the National Gallery of Umbria.

Galleria Nazionale dell' Umbria

The highlights of this huge collection of art, filling 33 rooms, are not always on display. Staff shortages, staff meetings (often a euphemism for a lightning strike or work-to-rule on the part of gallery attendants) and frequent rearrangements of the collection, often result in the closure of many rooms, and disappointment for the would-be visitor.

If you are fortunate enough to find the gallery open, you should seek out the acknowledged masterpieces of the Umbrian Renaissance; Fiorenzo di Lorenzo's lovely Adoration of the Shepherds (1490) and two paintings by Perugino: his Adoration of the Magi (c.1475–7), an early work which shows the definite influence of Botticelli (see the figure on the left, with a mop of curly hair standing hand on hip in the same posture in which Botticelli portrayed Lorenzo de' Medici in his own painting of this subject, now in the Uffizi Gallery, Florence); and his mature work, Christ Entombed, a stark and expressive painting of the dead Christ.

Seek out, too, the former Chapel of the Priors (Room 24), with its frescoes by Benedetto Bonfigli, illustrating the life of Perugia's patron saint, Bishop

Herculanus, who was martyred in AD547, after a seven-year-long siege of Perugia, at the hands of Totila the Goth.

Emerging back into Corso Vannucci, turn right and right again, through the tunnel that passes beneath the palace campanile to reach Via dei Priori.

Via dei Priori to the Piazza di San Francesco

This steep street leads downhill to the Oratorio de San Bernardino, but offers numerous distractions along the way. Characterful little medieval alleys lead off to either side, like the Via della Gabbia at the rear of the palace where criminals were once exposed in cages to the ridicule of the crowds. Down another alley, second on the left, is the tiny dark Gothic church of Sant' Agata, with its 14th-century *Crucifixion* fresco, painted on a midnight blue sky. Further down on the left is the Torre degli Sciri, a windowless and mono-lithic tower 46m high, named after the Sciri family and one of hundreds that used to bristle the skyline of Perugia.

Next, on the left, you pass the church of Madonna della Luce – the Madonna of the Light – its Renaissance façade with Corinthian pilasters and a pediment resembling a miniature Roman temple.

The church was built in 1513 to house a miraculous image of the Virgin, whose eyes closed and remained shut for four days after overhearing the blasphemies of an angry young barber who had lost a game of cards. If the church is open, look for the fresco of the *Madonna with Saints Francis and Ludovic* by Tiberio d'Assisi. To the left of the chapel, the Arco di San Luca (the Gate of St Luke) was part of the Etruscan city walls and marks the beginning of an ancient road that heads for Lake Trasimeno.

Finally, the narrow street opens out into the wide grass-covered plain of the Piazza di San Francesco, where the students of the nearby Academy of Fine Arts gather between lectures.

San Francesco al Prato

The first of the buildings flanking the square to catch the eye is the large church of San Francesco al Prato – St Francis in the Fields – so called because this Franciscan church was built on land that lay outside the city walls.

The church was begun around 1253, with a plan (aisleless nave, transepts and apse) identical to the basilica at Assisi. Many wealthy patrons of the Franciscan order are buried here, including Braccio Fortebraccio (Fortebraccio means Strongarm), the tough mercenary leader who succeeded in carving out a miniature kingdom for himself, which he ruled from Perugia, in the early 15th century.

You cannot, though, see these graves, for the church was built on unstable ground and numerous efforts to prevent subsidence and collapse, beginning as early as the 1400s, have failed to resolve the problem. The walls just about still stand and you can glimpse, through the windows, the bare ruined nave. Restoration, a slow and frequently interrupted process, is under way, and the façade at least can be enjoyed, with its delicate panelling of pink and white stone.

Oratorio di San Bernardino

To the left of the church is the entrance to the Accademia and, to the left of that, the Oratorio di San Bernardino, the real reason for coming here – for the façade is covered in reliefs that are among the most delightful in all of Italy.

The oratory was begun in 1451, the year after the canonisation of Saint Bernardino of Siena in whose honour it was built. In his lifetime the saint had done much to try and end the constant strife between rival Umbrian cities, and between bands of mercenaries led by despots like Fortebraccio who fought on their behalf.

Bernardino not only travelled about the countryside, preaching a message of peace and reconciliation, he also played a practical role in drawing up statutes for cities like Perugia which were intended to regulate local government and end the in-fighting. (Incidentally, in recognition of his persuasive tongue, Bernardino recently suffered the indignity of being declared the patron saint of advertising.)

Perugians remained notoriously fond of strife, but they nevertheless chose to honour the saint and commissioned the great Florentine sculptor, Agostino di Duccio, to decorate the oratory façade.

Duccio chose to place Saint Bernardino at the centre of a joyful band of heavenly musicians and choristers. The saint, carved on the tympanum, is the only still figure amongst a mass of joyful, dancing girls and cherubs, beating drums and triangles, playing viols, sackbuts and trumpets in a frenzy of celebration.

Much of the animation in this sculpture comes from the diaphanous drapery of the musicians which swirls and billows as if stirred by a heavenly wind. At the same time these figures are reminiscent of Donatello's figures carved on the choir loft made for Florence cathedral (which may well have inspired Duccio) and of the richly intricate figures in the Art Nouveau posters of Alphonse Mucha.

Immediately around the doorway itself Duccio carved the six Cardinal Virtues (Mercy, Holiness and Purity on the left and Religion, Mortification and Penance on the right). Above the door, San Bernardino is depicted preaching to the children of Perugia, flanked by scenes of his miracles. The corner niches contain statues of the Archangel Gabriel and Saint Constantius (left) and the Virgin and Saint Herculanus (right).

Inside the oratory, which was remodelled in the 17th century, the marble altar is a composite piece. The lower part consists of the 4th-century sarcophagus of St Egidio, the front panel divided by Corinthian columns into a series of niches; the central one encloses Christ in Majesty and the others contain

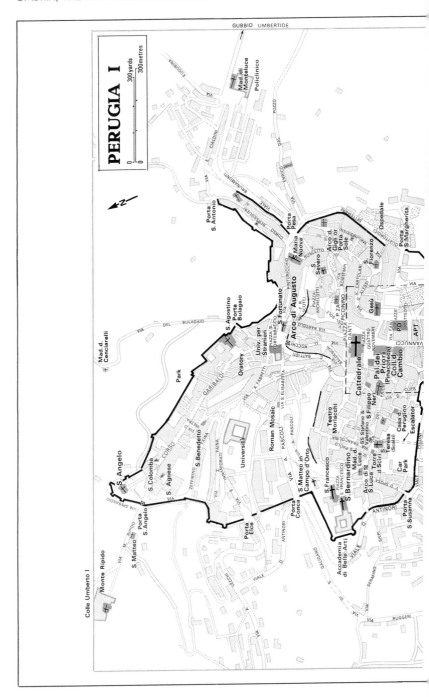

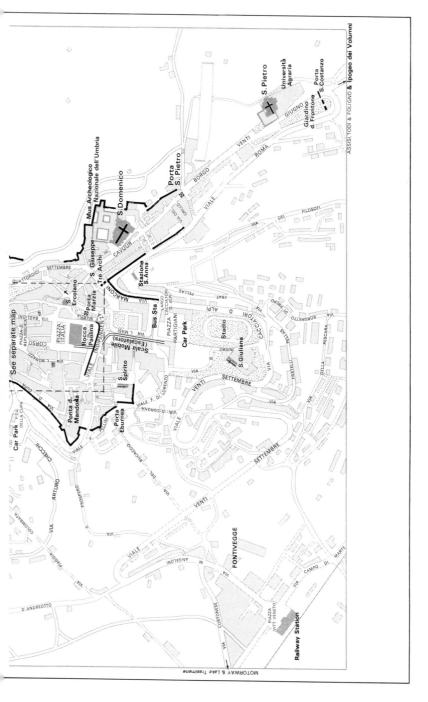

figures carrying scrolls who may represent the Virgin and Apostles. Above the tomb is a 14th-century frieze carved with the story of Jonah, whose return from the belly of the whale symbolises the Resurrection.

The northern quarter

The Via A. Pascoli, leading north out of the piazza, contains nothing of interest but leads swiftly to the Via del Acquedotto – best viewed from Via Appia which runs alongside to the left. As the name suggests, the Via del Acquedotto is a picturesque elevated walkway resting on arches that once carried Perugia's water supply from Monte Pacciano to the Fontana Maggiore in the main square.

Just to the south, Piazza Gallenga is dominated by the 18th-century Baroque Palazzo Gallenga that houses the Università Italiana per Stranieri – the University for Foreigners. Founded in 1926 by Mussolini, the University receives three thousand overseas students a year who come to study the Italian language, literature and culture. Many of them are from British or American universities. If you are staying in Perugia and want to know what is happening in the city, especially after dark, the foyer noticeboard is a good source of information, as is the convivial and cosmopolitan bar.

Alongside the University is the unmissable bulk of Perugia's best surviving city gate, known as the Etruscan Arch (Arco Etrusco) because the huge blocks of stone forming the two trapezoidal towers belong to the 3rd-century BC Etruscan defences. This was the main gate of seven that pierced the formidable walls, encircling the city with a total length of nearly 3km.

The upper level of the gate, with its arches, Ionic columns and frieze of shields, was added when the Romans conquered the city in 40BC. The city was then renamed Augusta Perusia. You can see the name carved within the arch: the name of the conquering emperor in large letters, that of the town in submissive small ones. Crowning the whole structure is a 16th-century loggia, its delicacy forming a poignant contrast with the monolithic structure below.

If, by this stage, you have had your fill of churches and monuments, you can return to the city centre in a matter of minutes by taking the Via Ulisse Rocchi. Nicknamed the Via Vecchio, because this was the main street of the Etruscan city and has therefore been in use for three millennia, the road leads uphill, directly back to the cathedral.

Otherwise, you can head east along the Corso Garibaldi. The ultimate objective is the 5th-century church of Sant' Angelo, but you might want to stop first to see the church of Sant' Agostino. This bulky church, with a 13th-century pink and white chequerboard façade, seems, at first, to hold nothing of interest within, but the wooden stalls of the choir are well worth a look. The gorgeous carving and inlay work was carried out by Baccio d'Angolo – possibly to designs drawn by Perugino – and took thirty years to complete, starting in 1502.

The Via del Acquedotto is a picturesque elevated watercourse, now dry

While you are here, look for the fresco depicting the Crucifixion in the second chapel on the left of the nave, painted by Pellino di Vannuccio in 1377. The remainder of the great works of art that this church once held were looted by Napoleon's army.

Alongside the church is the Oratorio della Confraternità di Sant' Agostino (Chapel of the Augustinian Brotherhood), one of the few examples of Baroque architecture in the region to deserve more than a dismissive glance. The correct architectural term is, perhaps, proto-Baroque, for the wonderful ceiling of carved and gilded wood dates to the first decade of the 17th century and is therefore earlier than most of the full-blown baroquery that mars so many churches. The work was executed by two French craftsmen, Charles d'Amuelle and Monsu Filippe. The carving, which frames 17th and 18th-century paintings, is scarcely religious at all: the intertwining branches, inhabited by putti, seem designed for a palace or opera house rather than a church.

Corso Garibaldi leads to the northernmost limits of the old city, and in the angle of the walls, at one of the highest points in Perugia, surrounded by cypress trees, you will find the circular Tempio di Sant' Angelo, the Temple of St Michael the Archangel.

Sant' Angelo

To appreciate the architecture of this church you have to separate the myth from the reality. Perugians like to believe that the church is built on the foundations of an Etruscan temple to the sun which dictated its circular form. In fact, the church dates from the 5th or 6th century and the plan emulates Byzantine-inspired early Christian churches, such as those of Rome and Ravenna.

The central polygonal space is separated from the ambulatory by a ring of marble pillars, rising to Corinthian-style capitals, all different and all, no doubt, salvaged from Roman buildings. Stripped of plaster, the construction of the rotunda is revealed; voussoirs of brick, perhaps also Roman, support walls of alternate courses of tile and stone. The vaults that now support the open timber roof are 13th-century. Though simple and lacking any great works of art, this church is nevertheless one of the most atmospheric in Perugia.

The convent of Sant' Agnese, almost opposite the Temple, can be visited only if you are accompanied by a nun. You may think the effort worthwhile to see one of Perugino's most lyrical frescoes. The *Crowned Madonna* was painted in 1522, towards the end of Perugino's life. The Virgin is portrayed in a peaceful and realistic landscape, and the two nuns kneeling either side were cousins of the artist, both nuns at this convent.

Returning up the Corso Garibaldi, you can divert left to the Porto Sperandio, and step through to the almost rural road beyond for a well-preserved stretch of the city's medieval walls.

From Piazza Fortebraccio the Piazza Danti

Back in the Piazza Fortebraccio, the most interesting route back to the cathedral is to head east along Via Pinturicchio, pausing at the church of Santa Maria Nuova, with its imposing 17th-century campanile. The church contains another gonfalone, or processional banner, painted by Benedetto Bonfigli in 1471. It shows an angry Christ hurling arrows down on to the citizens of Perugia, while various saints plead for the just citizens to be spared. The choir stalls are extraordinarily rich examples of mid 15th-century craftsmanship.

Via del Roscetto leads uphill, beneath an arch, to Via Bontempi and the little church of San Severo. This contains a damaged fresco, the work of Perugino (the lower tier of saints) and his pupil Raphael (Christ in Majesty, above). The dates of the fresco tell a poignant story. Raphael painted his portion in 1505, and it represents one of his earliest works. Perugino painted his in 1521; it is therefore one of his last works. It was executed, moreover, a year after Raphael's untimately death, at the age of 37, and not long before the end of Perugino's own life.

In Piazza Danti, just up from San Severo, and in the lee of the cathedral's west face, you can visit an Etruscan well: this massive stone-lined shaft, 35m deep and 5.6m across, dates to the 4th century BC.

Piazza Italia and the southern quarter

More ancient remains are to be found beneath Perugia's main street, although you would not realise this as you head away from the cathedral, down Corso Vannucci. The imposing buildings of Piazza Italia, which lie ahead, all date to the 19th century and are built on a platform that offers views for miles across the Perugian hinterland. Nothing more than a century old is in sight until you descend to the Via Marzia, at the foot of the Piazza Italia. Here, propping up the piazza, is the last surviving angle buttress of a once imposing fortress.

The Rocca Paolina was begun in 1530, built on the orders of Pope Paul III in order to control the rebellious city. Perugia had been torn by strife for seventy years as the two leading families, the Oddi and the Baglioni, fought for control and pursued their vendettas with ruthless tenacity. When not fighting their rivals, the families murdered each other; on one occasion the cathedral had to be cleansed with wine and reconsecrated after a particularly bloody massacre in which Grifonetto Baglioni sought to wipe out all his relatives, leaving him sole ruler of the city.

Matters came to a head when the papal legate was murdered in 1535. Paul III sent his troops to break the Baglioni family. Their palaces were destroyed, along with all that part of the city they controlled, almost a quarter of the city's total extent. The Rocca was then built on the ruins and the Pope continued to rule the city for the next 300 years. Papal troops brutally quashed the

Republican uprising in Perugia that took place in 1859. A year later, Perugians took their long-awaited revenge. Garibaldi's followers liberated the city in that year and the fortress was torn down.

Only the Porta Marzia was saved, partly because it incorporates the remains of a 3rd-century BC Etruscan city gate, decorated with the busts (all now headless bar one) of horses and Roman deities. Below this arch a narrow door leads into the Via Baglioni – a complete medieval street preserved in the subterranean depths of the fortress.

Steep narrow streets lead down from here to the long narrow spur forming the south-western suburbs of the city. On the corner of Via Oberdan and Via Marzia, a small garden fronts the octagonal church of Sant' Ercolano, built in 1326 on the spot where Bishop Herculanus, patron saint of Perugia, was decapitated by Totila the Goth.

San Domenico

Via Cavour, the ancient road to Assisi, leads from here to San Domenico. This massive church, begun in 1305, was never finished and presents a gaunt, rough-hewn façade to the world. The interior, so large that it once accommodated a whole regiment of Napoleonic troops and their horses, is now empty of furnishings. The great works of art once held here have been transferred to the National Gallery of Umbria, and replaced here and there by poor 19th-century paintings and Madonnas with electronically lit halos.

In the sanctuary a massive organ case, as ornate as a fairground piece, competes for attention with Italy's second largest stained glass window (the largest being that of Milan Cathedral), filled with figures of saints and dating from 1411.

Then, to the right of the high altar, you notice the exquisite and pristine tomb of Pope Benedict XI, rightly hailed as the best example of Gothic funerary sculpture in all Italy. Pope Benedict died in Perugia in 1304 after eating figs poisoned by an unknown enemy. The sculptor of this masterful monument is also unknown: some attribute it to Pisano but without any confirmatory evidence.

The tomb consists of a sarcophagus inset with four panels containing saints carved in high relief. Above we see, as through a church window, the Virgin and Child, flanked by the kneeling pope and a companion, and St Dominic. Below the sarcophagus, Pope Benedict is portrayed lying in repose as two angels draw together the curtains around his bed. The whole shrine is covered by a canopy supported on barley-sugar stick columns, studded with tiny figures clambering their way up to heaven.

Close by the tomb is another remarkable carving of another era: the realistic, and perhaps unflattering, bust of Elisabetta Cantucci de Colis, carved by Alessandro Algardi in 1648.

Chapels radiating from the apse have been less harmed by 18th-century reworking than the rest of the church. The Chapel of St Thomas has a vivid fresco depicting the killing of St Peter the Martyr by Cola Petruccioli (late 14th century) and another has richly coloured frescoes of the Virgin attributed to Benedetto Bonfigli.

The Banner Chapel, in the north aisle, contains a gonfalone by Giannicola di Paolo, showing the now familiar subject of Saints Dominic and Colomba protecting the citizens of Perugia from the wrath of God. This was commissioned in 1494 when the city was in the grip of a plague. In the opposite aisle, the Chapel of St Lawrence has an unusual altar frontal and reredos of stone and terracotta made by Agostino di Antonio di Duccio in 1459, depicting saints and miracles attributed to the Rosary.

The cloisters of San Domenico now house the National Archaeological Museum of Umbria. This is worth visiting if only for the fine views southwards over open countryside to be had from the museum's upper floors.

If you come here seeking objects to help you understand the mysterious Umbrians, the pre-Roman peoples whose territory began immediately east of Perugia, you will be disappointed, for they are represented only by a few fragments of crude early pottery. By contrast, the mass of Etruscan material provides a vivid picture of these people, whose territory extended westwards from Perugia, from the Tiber to the sea. The Etruscans were masters of bronze casting and some of the most impressive exhibits here are the mighty shields and pieces of armour, the delicate mirrors engraved with erotic scenes, great torques, bracelets, brooches and pendants, 23 centimetres or more across.

The picture that emerges is contradictory. There is armour aplenty and red or black-figure vases, Hellenistic in style, painted with scenes that glorify war. Yet there are also delicate balletic figures carved in stone, the dancers frozen in static poses where the movement is all conveyed through a gesture of the hands.

You come away puzzled by the paradox of a people at once so barbaric and bellicose and yet so cultured and artistic; and then you remember that Perugians have been just the same over the centuries, a people who were constantly at war with their neighbours and brawling amongst themselves and yet who managed to create a city filled with outstanding architecture and art.

San Pietro

San Pietro is the last stop on the itinerary. The tall six-sided campanile, topped by a spire, is visible from most parts of the city and San Pietro could claim to be the most rewarding church in Perugia, though few visitors venture this far from the centre. The entrance is through the graceful north cloister, whose buildings now serve as Perugia University's Faculty of Agriculture. Frescoes of the 13th and 14th centuries, showing the *Annunciation*, *St George and the Dragon* and *Christ Entombed*, flank the portal.

Inside, every surface beneath the gilded and coffered roof is covered in colour. The overall effect is magnificent, although not all the work is of equal merit. The 11 giant canvases framed on the upper walls of the nave, by Vassilacchi and painted in Venice in 1593–4, are didactic and academic. Pleasure comes from the less monumental details, especially the nave arcades,

7. THE VALE OF SPOLETO

From Perugia the busy N75 curves south eastwards to Foligno where it joins the N3, the ancient Roman Via Flaminia, and heads due south to Spoleto. This road follows the eastern shore of an extinct lake. Like Lake Trasimeno today, that former lake was never very deep. Deliberate drainage began under the Romans and by 1600 the lake had virtually dried up completely.

Factories making foodstuffs – chocolate, biscuits and pasta – offices and housing suburbs have now colonised the former swamps, and the view from the plain can sometimes be dispiriting. The spirits lift again, however, as soon as you divert off the main road to seek out the spectacular hilltop towns that are strung out at regular intervals, like pearls on a rope, along the rim of the Vale.

Spello and Foligno

The first of these is **SPELLO**, an ancient Umbrian settlement chosen by Augustus as a place of retirement for veterans of his military campaigns. Roman Hispellum was demarcated by a wall, some 2km in circumference, and modern Spello, a town of just over 1000 inhabitants, has scarcely grown beyond this boundary.

The walls, with their polygonal angle turrets, still stand to an impressive height, defining the shape of the town as it climbs up the narrow shoulder of a hill beneath Monte Subasio.

You enter through the Roman **Porta Venere**, flanked by 12th-century towers and named after a nearby temple to Venus, which has not survived. In the vicinity of the gate your eye quickly learns to distinguish the Roman from the medieval masonry in the surrounding buildings. In the lower courses, the regular blocks of stone are all of a similar size, squared off with military precision. Higher up the medieval masons used undressed, round-edged stones of many sizes, skilfully interlocking the irregular surfaces to create a solid and stable wall.

Santa Maria Maggiore

Further into the town medieval predominates, with a bit of Roman carving reused here and there as decoration. Two fluted Roman columns, for example, stand by the pink campanile of Santa Maria Maggiore (Piazza Matteotti) and pieces of Roman frieze are incorporated into the striking portal, made in 1644. This also incorporates lively 13th-century masonry, carved with birds and beasts hidden amongst the acanthus-leaf scroll.

Just inside the door you stumble across more Roman masonry. The holy water stoop on the left is made from a Corinthian capital. That on the right is a splendid tombstone, with a hollowed-out top, to a Roman cavalier, carved with a relief of a soldier on horseback and of birds feeding from a fig tree, symbol of immortality.

The dull baroquery of the rest of the church disappoints until you notice the frescoes in the Cappella Baglioni on the left of the nave. Switching on the lights transforms this gloomy chapel into a blaze of glorious colour. Pinturicchio was a pupil of, and later collaborator with, Perugino. Vasari is somewhat dismissive of his work, accusing him of too much prettiness, designed to 'satisfy those who understand little about art and give them more show and lustre, which is a barbarous thing to do in painting'.

Subsequent critics, taking their lead from Vasari, have said much the same thing but few people standing in front of these scenes can fail to be delighted, even if it means being counted as one who understands little about art. Painted in 1501, they represent the *Annunciation*, the *Nativity*, the *Coming of the Magi*, the *Dispute in the Temple* and the *Sybils who Foretold the Birth of Christ*.

Restoration has revealed the true sensuality of the colours, the exotic landscape full of fascinating detail, the grouping and expressive gestures of the figures and the fully realised perspective (best appreciated by standing well back from the walls, even on the opposite side of the nave). The artist, no doubt proud of his own work, left a self-portrait hanging on the wall of the house in which the Archangel Gabriel appears to the Virgin.

The floor of the chapel also contributes to the rich effect. The 16th-century majolica tiles, made in Deruta on the opposite side of the Vale, are painted with dragons and griffins. They are worn but, here and there, a patch of colour stands out with the brilliance and intricacy of a Persian carpet.

When the lights go out the world suddenly seems a duller place and there are few other treasures in the church. There is another serene *Madonna and Child* by Pinturicchio in the chapel to the left of the apse and two late, and sadly uninspired, works by Perugino – a *Pietà* and a *Madonna and Child*, dated 1521 – either side of the altar.

The rest of Spello is quickly explored. If you are not sated by Madonnas you should seek out another restored fresco by Pinturicchio (1508) in the simple church of Sant' Andrea, a short step further up Via Cavour behind the early morning street market. The Piazza Comunale in the Piazza della Repubblica has a small art gallery whose highlight is Petruccioli's *Crucifixion* and *Coronation of the Virgin*. A stiff climb to the Belvedere at the highest point in the town is rewarded by views down on to the remains of the Roman amphitheatre and over to Perugia.

Foligno, the next town south, is an optional stop. War-time bombing and post-war growth has compromised the original character of the medieval town, which now survives only in fragments – notably the 13th-century south face of the cathedral, carved with zodiacal signs, real and imaginary beasts and a figure said to represent the Holy Roman Emperor, Frederick II.

On the other hand, the peaceful **Abbazia di Sassovivo**, just under 6km east of the town up a steep mountain road, should not be missed. The chances are that you will be the sole visitor to this small Benedictine monastery, founded in 1070, with its gracious Romanesque cloister set in a woodland clearing.

Trevi to Spoleto

Trevi

At Trevi the modern world is left behind again as you step within the walls. Streets too narrow and steep for motor cars have been turned into minor works of art, paved with pebbles set in frames of stone or brick to divide the surfaces into patterns of squares, diamonds or herringbone. Few streets are straight and you never know what to expect around the next turning: ancient buildings pierced by medieval archways that offer glimpses of shady, flower-filled courtyards, oversailing buttresses and massive corbels (sporti) holding up the jettied upper storeys of sombre palazzi. The sky is scarcely visible and the town remains cool in the shadows cast by the tall and closely spaced buildings, unlike the baking hot and modern suburban sprawl outside the town walls.

The maze of alleys leads you upwards to the highest point in the town. Here, in the Via Placido Riccardi, the church of **Sant' Emiliano** provides both pleasure and disappointment. The campanile, which looks so splendid from a distance, like a pinnacle rising above the red-brown rooftops of the town, turns out to be made of utilitarian yellow brick.

The church itself has a lovely Romanesque exterior with a cluster of chapels around the apse, but the interior has been comprehensively ruined by dull sub-classical remodelling in the 18th and 19th centuries. One earlier feature has survived; the splendid altar in the north aisle, shaped like a triumphal arch and covered in grotesque work, with a niche containing a realistic *Virgin and Child* – all the work of Mattia di Gaspare da Como and dating from 1524.

Back on the Via Flaminia, amongst the traffic thundering south to Rome, it is easy to miss the signpost to the **Tempio di Clitunno**. If you do miss it, turn round and head north again, for this is one of Umbria's earliest and most fascinating churches, set in a lovely spot beside the clear waters of the River Clitunno.

Known locally as the 'tempietto', the little temple, the church looks like a mini Parthenon. It was built in the 4th or 5th century and is dedicated to the early Christian martyr, San Salvatore. Frescoes inside, now indistinct, date from the 7th or 8th century and are among the earliest to have survived in Italy. They depict Christ with Saints Peter and Paul.

It is less easy to miss the **Fonti del Clitunno**, the source of the River Clitunno, just 1km south, because it is fronted by a large restaurant and car park. Even the volume of visitors does not, however, destroy the magic of this spot where the pure spring waters gush, with some force, from clefts in the rock to spill into a willow-fringed pool.

The nymphs have long been driven away, the river god Clitunnus no longer issues oracles from the depths of the pool and sacrificial white bulls are no longer brought here for purification; even so, the spring waters remain crystal clear and water weeds grow erect in the still pool like a miniature underwater forest. Countless visitors, from Virgil and the Emperor Claudius, from the artist Corot to the poet Byron, have been charmed by the idyllic scene.

Spoleto

Spoleto, 11km south, brings a rude return to traffic congestion and the problems of parking; try the northern end of the city, the first part you encounter as you leave the Via Flaminia. Entered from this direction Spoleto does not present an attractive face. The scruffy Piazza di Vittorio is used as a racetrack by youths on their noisy *motorini*.

Ignoring the advice of local guide books to visit the Roman bridge hidden beneath this square, built to carry the Via Flaminia over the now dry Torrente Tessino and a rather sorry sight. Seek out instead the church of **San Gregorio Maggiore** on the west side of the piazza. This fascinating church has been restored to its 12th-century appearance. The upper façade is decorated with statues of priests in vestments while the Renaissance loggia below, built of reused Roman masonry, bears an inscription dedicated to Spoleto's 10,000 martyrs. These were the companions of St Abbondanza who, according to local tradition, were massacred in the nearby amphitheatre causing the Torrente Tessino to run red with their blood. St Abbondanza is buried within the church and the legend of her numerous companions in death might date to the 16th century, since the loggia, added as an afterthought, was not built until then. Sheltered by the loggia, the chapel on the left is frescoed with scenes depicting the Massacre of the Innocents, another allusion to the mythical massacre of Spoleto.

The interior of the church is beautiful in its simplicity. Following the basilican plan, the altar is raised on a dais 3m above the nave. Beneath this the

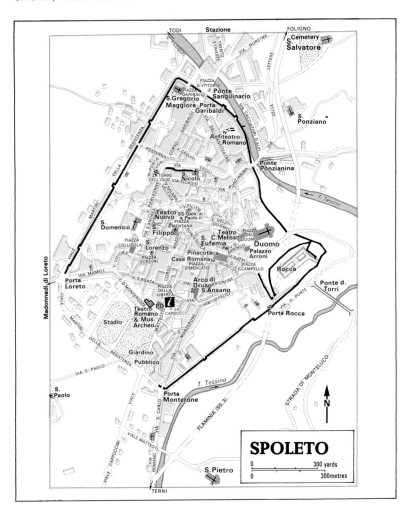

vaulted crypt contains a forest of reused Roman columns and capitals and the large sarcophagus of St Abbondanza.

You can still see the amphitheatre where the saint met her end on the left of the dreary Via dell' Anfiteatro, behind the severe façade of the former barracks. The nearly empty military buildings are now forlorn and the amphitheatre itself is dilapidated, consisting principally of the perimeter vault and the broken remains of stone seating. Much of the stone was stolen to build the city's fortress in the 14th century.

Piazza del Duomo

Via dell' Anfiteatro continues its characterless course uphill until, by total contrast, you enter the square in front of the cathedral, one of Umbria's most striking piazzas. To appreciate the full grace of beauty of the cathedral façade, you should walk away to the opposite end of the wide piazza or to the *murricciola*, the long stone bench that runs along the foot of the wall on the south side of the square.

Several ages have contributed to the making of this elegant building. The campanile, built of regular blocks of Roman masonry, and the upper façade both date to 1198, when Innocent III consecrated the new cathedral, built on the ruins of the old one, destroyed by the imperial troops of Frederick Barbarossa.

Eight rose windows, like lace doilies, pierce the façade. The central one is contained in a square frame supported by two caryatids, with symbols of the Evangelists carved in the corners. Above this window the mosaic of *Christ Enthroned with the Virgin and St John* is signed and dated 'Solsternus, 1207'. Beneath, the Renaissance portico with its two external, shell-hooded pulpits, dates from 1491.

Sadly, the interior comes as an anticlimax. Look up, as you enter the church, at the bust by Bernini of Pope Urban VIII; he was to blame for remodelling the cathedral in 1644. His architect, Luigi Arrigucci, did at least spare the lovely floor of inlaid marble and Filippo Lippi's frescoes in the sanctuary.

On your way to the sanctuary you will pass the Erioli Chapel, on the right, named after two bishops of Spoleto, with its *Madonna and Child* by Pinturicchio and sky blue ceiling painted by Jacopo Santori in the 16th century.

Filippo Lippi's **frescoes** (under restoration) were the last he ever did. Almost anyone who loves art will remember, either from reading Vasari or Browning's dramatic monologues, that Lippi was a colourful character – a wayward orphan whose aunt abandoned him to the care of Carmelite friars, at the age of eight, because she found him impossible to control.

Lippi's artistic talent was stimulated by his love of women. As Vasari recounts:

> Fra Filippo Lippi was so lustful that he would give anything to enjoy a woman he wanted if he thought he could have his way; and if he couldn't buy what he wanted, then he would cool his passion by painting her picture.

Thus Lippi is best known for his sensuous Virgins, many of them portraits of his mistress, the beautiful Lucrezia Buti, and familiar from countless Christmas cards.

Lippi was invited to Spoleto in 1468 with a commission to paint more Virgins; in fact a whole *Life of the Virgin*, from the *Annunciation* to the *Nativity* to her *Coronation in Heaven*. Lippi died before he could complete the work, aged fifty-seven. Vasari, who loved gossip, reports:

> they say that, in one of those sublime love affairs he was always having, the relations of the woman concerned had him poisoned.

Whether this is true or not, the artist died at the full height of his powers and now that these frescoes have been restored we are once again be able to enjoy the lyrical and tender figures and the vibrant colours that were his trademark.

When Lippi died the young Lorenzo de' Medici came to Spoleto to ask for the return of his body so that it could be buried in his native Florence. The people of Spoleto asked instead that Lippi remain with them, on the grounds that 'Florence had countless famous citizens, almost a superfluity, and so it could do without this one'; whereas 'Spoleto lacked any great marks of distinction and especially the adornment of eminent men.'

In a gesture of magnanimity unusual for the time, Spoleto was allowed to keep Lippi's remains and the Medici bank even donated one hundred gold ducats for a tomb; this was designed by Lippi's illegitimate son, himself by now an accomplished artist. The tomb is found in the right-hand transept, carved with an epigram written by the humanist orator, Politian. The last lines, translated, read:

> *Nature herself, as I revealed her, owned*
> *In wonderment that I could match her arts.*
> *Beneath the lowly soil was I interred*
> *Ere this; but now Lorenzo Medici*
> *Hath laid me here in this marble tomb.*

There is an ironical twist to the end of the story. The tomb no longer stands over Lippi's vault, and nobody now knows where his remains lie. During Pope Urban VIII's refurbishment of the cathedral, the relics of the only distinguished man Spoleto could call its own were simply lost.

Spoletans were less careless about one or two other relics. The chapel beneath the organ loft contains a 12th-century icon of the Virgin, said to have been looted from Constantinople by Frederick Barbarossa and given to Spoleto as a peace token in 1185, after the Emperor had destroyed the town. Further up the nave, on the right as you leave, is a Crucifixion painted on wood, dating from 1887, and a beautiful set of mid 16th-century stalls in the same chapel.

The **Museo Civico** (open 10.00–12.00, 15.00–17.00) is on the right-hand side of the Piazza del Duomo, housed in the Palazzo della Signoria, next to an elegant octagonal chamber theatre, the Caio Melisso, built in 1880. The museum contains an enjoyable miscellany of architectural fragments and 12th- to 15th-century sarcophagi. Two stone tablets, dating to the 3rd century BC, record the Lex Spoletina, a law forbidding the cutting of timber in the sacred groves around the city.

Climbing the steep steps out of the piazza, you should look back for a memorable view of the cathedral set against the distant wooded slopes, with the **Rocca** towering above it to the right. At the top of the steps, you can turn left to follow the Via della Rocca and come closer to this monumental fortress.

Totila the Goth first built a castle here in the 6th century, using Roman masonry looted from the Roman amphitheatre. The amphitheatre again served as a source for the 14th-century Rocca, once the most powerful in Umbria, and the base from which papal representatives subjugated the region. It was built in 1355, under the direction of Cardinal Albornoz, and, in more peaceful times, was converted to a luxurious palace, the home, for a time, of Lucrezia and Cesare Borgia, and a favourite papal retreat.

More recently, the Rocca has served as a maximum security prison, holding the Pope's would-be assassin and members of the Red Brigade. Now under restoration, it will soon reopen both as a museum housing the city's art collection and as a cultural centre intended as the focus of the Festival dei Due Mondi.

The reason for coming here now is the view over the spectacular **Ponte delle Torri**, the extraordinary acqueduct that spans the gorge between Monte Sant' Elia, on which the Rocca is built, and Monteluco, opposite. The Ponte was built in 1345, before the Rocca, but subsequently incorporated into it, serving the dual purpose of providing a reliable water supply in the event of siege and an escape route out of the city in extremis.

Water no longer flows along its channel (though it can be turned on if necessary) and it is possible to walk across the top of the massive structure, 230m long and 80m high, to the wooded slopes of Monteluco, enjoying the views up and down the Tessino gorge.

Back in the centre of Spoleto, just beyond the cathedral steps, in Via Aurelio Saffi, look for a gate in the wall on the right, leading into the quiet courtyard of the 15th-century Palazzo Arcivescovile. On the right of the courtyard is the simple façade of Sant' Eufemia, another of Spoleto's ancient and well-restored churches.

Sant' Eufemia stands on foundations that date from the 3rd century. Late Roman materials were used to build the current church in the 12th century and the ornate square column on the right-hand side of the nave, carved with patterns of vine leaves, may have come from the palace of the 8th-century Lombard Dukes of Spoleto. The triforium above was added in the 15th century and the matroneum, or women's gallery, at the west end in the 16th.

Emerging again from the grounds of the Archepiscopal Palace, turn right then first left, down to the Piazza del Municipio. This small square has one of several pieces of modern sculpture dotted about the city as a legacy of the Festival dei Due Mondi, standing in front of the **Palazzo Communale** which houses the city's picture gallery (open 10.00–13.00, 16.30–19.30, closed Tues).

Here, amongst the many anonymous and unlabelled paintings, you will find two works by Lo Spagna: *The Virtues* (1512) and a *Madonna and Child* (1516). Few other works of this accomplished artist survive in Umbria (the rest are scattered around the world's museums) even though he spent much of his working life in the region and absorbed the techniques of Perugino and Raphael to create his own influential style. The vaults of the palazzo contain the well-preserved remains of a 1st-century AD Roman house, once claimed to be the home of Vespasia Pollo, the mother of the Emperor Vespasian.

To the left of the Piazza del Municipio, as you emerge, you discover the busy shopping and restaurant centre of the city, the Piazza del Mercato. This stands on the site of the Roman forum and from here westwards and southwards the city is largely modern in date, rebuilt after the bombing of World War II.

This lower part of the town contains no compelling monuments but if you are bent on a comprehensive tour you should cross the square to the 1st-century AD **Arco di Druso**, spanning the southern exit. This was built to commemorate the Germanic victories of Drusus, son of the Emperor Tiberius. The somewhat sad and neglected remains of a Roman temple stand alongside, and more of the temple is incorporated into the crypt of Sant' Ansano, which also has some well-restored 12th-century frescoes.

Just to the south, off Piazza della Libertà, are the remains of the Roman theatre, largely rebuilt after the war and used for outdoor concerts and drama during the summer festival. The first turning left, Via Sant' Agata, leads you to the lovely 13th-century church of **San Domenico**, all of pink and white banded stone, a little touch of gracefulness amongst the drabber colours of post-war Spoleto.

Further out, in the south-western suburbs, is the church of **San Paolo** with endearing 13th-century frescoes of the creation of Adam and Eve. Nearby, the long Viale Martiri della Resistenza runs parallel to a well-preserved stretch of city wall and back to the Piazza della Vittoria.

Two of the best of Spoleto's churches, however, are yet to come. Both lie outside the city walls. The church of **San Salvatore** is located to the north of Piazza della Vittoria in the city cemetery. The siting of this 4th-century church is no accident; the very earliest churches often took the form of a martyrium, a mausoleum or funerary shrine to a leading member of the local Christian community. What is surprising is the survival of this church at all, and the fact that its existence suggests the cemetery has been in continuous use for 1700 years.

San Salvatore is a curious hybrid. The façade, with its pedimented windows, looks almost domestic; in fact one might even be looking at a very rare survival, a late Roman house. The interior is like a small Roman temple with the difference that none of the salvaged Roman columns used in its construction are the same. The apse, added 1000 years later, and some fragmentary frescoes are the only indication that this building had an ecclesiastical use.

Richard Krautheimer (*Early Christian and Byzantine Architecture*, Penguin, 1965) gives us an idea of the function of these early martyria, of which this is a particularly splendid example. He suggests that cemetery churches were used exclusively for funeral banquets. Separate churches were used for the rite of Baptism and for the celebration of Communion. Only later did one building come to serve all three functions.

Thus we have to try and imagine San Salvatore as a banqueting hall, a place

San Salvatore in Spoleto, dates to the 4th century and is one of the earliest churches to survive anywhere in Italy

Devils dismember the body of a sinner as St Michael walks away; carving on the façade of San Pietro church, Spoleto

in which to celebrate the passage of one or another member of Spoleto's early Christian community into an afterlife of eternal happiness. Interestingly, such funeral banquets were not a Christian innovation. The ancient Etruscans held similar rites, and their tombs are frequently carved with the figure of the deceased, reclining on a couch with a wine cup in one hand.

Equally intriguing is the thought that not all early Christian martyrs died a victim to persecution for their religion. In some cases the martyrium was built to honour a significant benefactor, some wealthy person who, true to the Christian ethic of Charity, had bequeathed their wealth to the fledgling church. Their feast day, initially, was exactly that; a once-a-year banquet held in their memory; in time, no doubt, as the memory of the real person grew dim, saintly or heroic deeds were attributed to their name.

San Salvatore is now a rather forlorn church, little visited and its dusty floor littered with the broken fragments of ancient masonry. By contrast, **San Pietro**, south of the city, buzzes with visitors. Its situation, by the side of the Via Flaminia, now a superstrada, ensures that it catches the eye of every passer-by. Moreover, the car park in front of the church provides a perfect vantage point for viewing the ten massive arches of the Ponte delle Torri, with the Rocca rising high to the left of the Tessino gorge.

San Pietro may once have been a martyrium as well, for it stands on the site of an ancient cemetery. In the 5th century it was used to house the relics of St Peter's chain, stolen from Rome by Bishop Achillus. That relic has since gone back to Rome and the church has been rebuilt several times, most notably in 1393, following a fire.

The façade must have survived that fire for, though nobody is certain of the precise dates, the lively carving around the portal belongs, stylistically, to the late 12th or early 13th century. The portal itself is surrounded by a delicate floral frieze enclosing panels of blank arcading and symbolic beasts: peacocks for immortality, a deer suckling her young and killing a viper – perhaps a homely, rural allegory of God's love and protection – and a ploughman in a tunic working the fields with the help of two oxen – perhaps symbolising the toil of Adam.

Ten larger panels flank the doorway, encapsulating medieval beliefs in a highly accomplished form of strip cartoon. On the top left-hand side, St Peter and an archangel stand guard over the bed of a dying man while a devil seated between them looks angry and holds up a placard inscribed 'Doleo Quia Ante Erat Meus' (I grieve because he was mine before). The scene below presents the antithesis: two devils dismember the body of an unrepentant sinner and throw the bits into a cauldron as the archangel departs.

The next three allegorical scenes all feature a lion. In the first the lion's paw is caught in a cleft in a tree which is being felled by a forester; in the second a man is kneeling in reverence before the lion; in the third the lion is attacking a knight in armour. It is difficult to interpret the meaning in any consistent way. The lion may represent the mercy and the wrath of God in the last two panels, but the first scene remains a mystery; perhaps God here is the axeman rescuing the lion from the ensnarement of sin.

The top two scenes on the right-hand side are immediately recognisable as Christ washing the feet of St Peter and calming the stormy waters of Lake Tiberias. The next two panels illustrate episodes from one of the popular medieval beast epics, perhaps the satirical *Roman de Renard*. In the first, Reynard the Fox feigns death in order to ensnare two crows; in the second he is disguised in a monastic cowl and turns from the book he is studying to eye his potential victim, a ram. Finally the lion appears again, chasing a dragon, probably representing God and Satan.

These panels are carved with great skill and their naturalism, especially in the agricultural scenes, is charming. The rest of the church is depressingly Baroque, rebuilt in 1699, and not worth even a fleeting glance. Instead leave Spoleto by the station road, turning left just before the station itself, and follow the well-signposted road through the suburbs towards Montefalco.

South to Bevagna

The road today follows the opposite, western, shores of the dried-up lake, now given over to regular plots of neat fields where tobacco, maize and sunflowers are the major crops.

Along the way you will pass the romantic castle ruins of **Castel Ritaldi**, on the left, and the unromantic modern water tower on the approach road to Montefalco itself.

Montefalco

The views from the walls of this town are so extensive that Montefalco has been dubbed the *ringhiera*, or balcony, of Umbria but they do not, thanks to careful siting, take in the water tower. Usually, too, the industrial suburbs of Foligno, on the opposite side of the Vale, are obscured by haze.

In the church of Sant' Agostino, on the main street, Corso G. Mameli, there is a fresco which shows the view as it was in the 15th century. The Madonna with Saints Augustine and Nicholas is attributed to Ugolino di Gisberto. The background shows the view from Montefalco to Foligno, the artist's native town, pretty much as it is today with the exception that there is still water in the lake in Gisberto's painting.

Another church nearby, in Via Verdi, is dedicated to Santa Chiara – a local girl who died in 1308, not the founder of the Poor Clares. If you ask the nuns in the adjacent convent they will show you a tree that grew from a staff given by Christ to Santa Chiara in a vision. The nuns used the dried berries of this tree to make rosary beads. The convent has several other relics of the saint, including the remains of her heart which was discovered, after her death, to be marked with a cross.

These are diversions from the town's main attraction, the church of **San Francesco**, founded in 1336 but deconsecrated in 1890 and turned into a museum for the display of Franciscan art: works either given to or commissioned by the order (open 10.00–13.00, 15.00–18.00, closed Thurs).

Without doubt, the highlight of the museum is the *in situ* fresco cycle in the sanctuary, painted by the Florentine artist Benozzo Gozzoli between 1450 and 1452. The 12 scenes from the life of St Francis are not as well known as Giotto's work, but they are easier to enjoy. You do not, as with Giotto, have to make allowances for the lack of sophistication, for Gozzoli was an artist working with the whole range of new techniques that had been developed by Florentine Renaissance artists, including Gozzoli's own teacher, Fra Angelico.

What makes these works even more appealing is the realistic background detail, much of it corresponding to recognisable scenes and buildings that survive to this day. Thus anyone who knows Florence will recognise that the 'church' in the vision of St Francis (below the central window) is in fact the Palazzo Vecchio, but given an extra campanile. St Peter's church in Rome features in the sixth scene, the meeting between Saints Francis and Dominic, and Montefalco itself features in the best scene of all, to the right of the window, in which St Francis preaches to the birds.

The only works in the museum that compare in quality to those of Gozzoli are the two paintings at the rear of the north aisle. Here, two versions of the *Madonna and Child* are set side by side to invite comparisons. One is by Tiberio d'Assisi (1510), the other by Perugino (1515). Both are beautifully fresh and the colour range – purples, oranges, glowing reds and irridescent blues – is quite arresting.

In the opposite aisle, in the two easternmost chapels, are two gonfalone portraying the Madonna del Soccorso (the Madonna of Assistance); one is anonymous (dated to around 1498) and the other is by Tiberio d'Assisi (1510). Both are highly comical and illustrate a popular local legend according to which a mother, exasperated by the bad behaviour of her child, wished him to the devil. The devil duly turned up to carry the child away so the distraught mother turned to the Virgin for help. In both paintings the Virgin is far from being the tender mother portrayed in most paintings; she is a club-wielding giantess from Umbrian folklore, fierce enough to frighten any devil or any disobedient child.

Bevagna

The last stop before returning to Assisi or Perugia is the little town of Bevagna, a quiet unspoiled gem of a town that is likely to furnish as many memories as any of its bigger neighbours.

The tree-lined Piazza Garibaldi lies just within the town walls. To the right, in the basement of Via Porta Guelfa 2, you will find a well-preserved Roman bath-house mosaic, featuring the sea-god Triton and an entourage of dolphins, octopus, sea-horses and a delightfully realised lobster.

A little further along, in Via S Crescimbeni, are the scant remains of a Roman temple, a reminder that Bevagna – Roman Mevania – was a thriving town, bigger than the present one, in the 1st and 2nd centuries AD. Then the town was famous for breeding Umbria's famous sacred white bulls, whose deer-like features made them highly prized as participants in religious ceremonies, usually to end up as sacrificial victims on an altar to Juno or Jupiter. It was also the birthplace of the poet Propertius, who described his native town as 'cloudy Mevania, standing among rain-soaked fields'.

The sleepy main street of today's town, the Corso Matteotti, leads (right) into the main square, the **Piazza Silvestri**. This delightful square has scarcely any buildings later than the 13th century and it demonstrates the pride that the medieval citizens took in their status as an independent commune. The status was continually under attack; Bevagna was destroyed by the Goths in the 6th century, by Frederick Barbarossa in the 12th, by his grandson Frederick II in the 13th and by the army of neighbouring Foligno in the 14th.

After each sacking the Bevagnans patched up their buildings, which now present a rough and ready but endearing appearance. To the left of the square, the elegant fountain was remade in the 19th century but faithful to the 13th-century original. A broad flight of stairs leads up one side of the Palazzo dei Consoli, the town's most elegant building, built in 1270 and now housing the splendid Teatro Torti. Look inside if you can; for the theatre, founded in 1886, has recently been restored to its 19th-century glory.

Alongside stands the church of **San Silvestro** with its broken roofline and stump of unfinished campanile. Built of Roman masonry, the name of the architect, Binello, and the date, 1195, are carved in the inscription to the right of the portal. The church is almost windowless and dark, as if to heighten

Good and evil in combat on the portal of San Michele church, Bevagna

the sense of mystery surrounding the rituals of the medieval Church. Binelli's columns in the nave have intrigued architectural historians; carved with a papyrus-like motif, they wonder if Binelli had seen some long-ruined ancient Roman temple to an eastern deity – perhaps Isis – and copied its capitals.

Directly opposite, the church of San Michele again bears an inscription: 'Rodolfus Binellu Fecet' (Rodolfo and Binello made this). The same two architects were later to build the south façade of Foligno cathedral and here their growing confidence as architects is evident in the carvings of the façade, interspersed between reused Roman egg-and-dart mouldings.

Two lively angels guard the portal. One bears the scriptures and thrusts a spear into the mouth of a dragon; the other carries an orb and crucifix. The corbel table above is carved with grotesque beasts. Pairs of Romanesque triple lancets light the aisles. The rose window, too large in proportion to the rest of the façade, is an unfortunate 18th-century addition, but the 17th-century wooden tympanum, showing the Archangel Michael casting Lucifer from Heaven, is in sympathy with the original architects' work. Inside, the nave is very tall, long and narrow, focussing attention on the altar, raised by some 3m above the floor. The nave is separated from the aisles by an eight-bay arcade of great elegance, supported on travertine pillars, sadly hacked about in the 18th century when the columns and walls were plastered over. Restoration in 1954 has given back to San Michele something of its original appearance, and the simplicity of this ancient church is just as pleasing as any more gorgeously frescoed one.

A third church in the square is dedicated to Sts Domenico and Giacomo. It has been given the Baroque treatment but remains surprisingly light and airy, with *trompe l'oeil* painted side altars instead of real ones and a fine porphyry east window, made of black and rust-coloured marble, planed as thin as eggshell.

Practical Information

Tourist Information Offices

BEVAGNA   Piazza Silvestri.

SPELLO   Via Garibaldi 17.

SPOLETO   Piazza della Libertà 7.

Where to stay

MONTEFALCO
Nuovo Mondo, Via Mameli 67 (tel. 0742-79243: Small, quiet and with a swimming pool.

SPOLETO
Gattapone, Via del Ponte 6 (tel. 0743-36147): A tiny hotel but very popular for its outstanding views over the Ponte delle Torri and the Tessino Gorge.
Dei Duchi, Viale Matteotti 4 (tel. 0743-44541): Central and popular with festival-goers and performers.
Dell' Angelo, Via Arco di Druso 25 (tel. 0743-32185): Small, central and cheap.

Where to eat

SPELLO
Il Molino, Piazza Matteotti 6, (tel. 0742-651305): Highly regarded by local people with a vaulted medieval dining room and specialising in meats roasted over an open fire (closed Tues).

SPOLETO
Il Tartufo, Piazza Garibaldi 24 (tel. 0743-40236): The top restaurant in Spoleto and the place to go for authentic Umbrian dishes and to spot internationally renowned artists during the festival – if you can afford it.
Sabatini, Corso Mazzini 52 (tel. 0743-37233): The same Umbrian specialities but more affordable, and with a large garden for summer dining.
La Cantina, Via Filitteria 10a (tel. 0743-44475): An excellent wine bar serving Umbrian snacks (closed Tues).

8. FROM PERUGIA TO ORVIETO

Deruta and Todi

The town of Deruta, just south of Perugia at the end of a picturesque stretch of the Tiber valley, is given over almost entirely to the production and sale of majolica. The long main street is lined with workshops and showrooms and you can choose between those that specialise in reproductions (*reproduzione* or *tradizione*) and those that produce more contemporary designs (*artistiche* or *moderne*).

If you want to see the complete range of ceramics under one roof you should visit the **Museo Regionale della Ceramica** in the Palazzo Communale (Piazza dei Consoli, open 9.00–13.00, closed Sun), where the exhibits range from the earliest to the most modern pieces.

Faenza is the name that springs most readily to mind when we think of majolica, and that city dominated early production, beginning in the 13th century. Once in command of the formulae for producing tin glaze, and the various bright underglaze colours that make majolica so distinctive, potters from Faenza were only too happy to move elsewhere and seek profitable new markets.

In Deruta, potters found deposits of clay containing the glassy, sandy silicate essential to their craft. The earliest records of pottery production here date to 1387 and the earliest surviving pieces, dating to the end of the 15th century, show the definite influence of Faenza in their colours and designs.

Gradually the Derutans began to develop their own style, specialising in monumental plates and vases, characterised by their heavy relief moulding. Grotesque ornament, fruit and foliage scrolls are typical Derutan motifs and the predominant colours, particularly during the 16th century when the local industry was at its most creative, are rich deep yellow and an almost turquoise blue.

Deruta's own museum has few of the most splendid Renaissance pieces – these are now spread across the globe in major collections – but it does have a very fine majolica tile floor, taken from the church of San Francesco and dating to 1524.

San Francesco stands close by the museum; rebuilt after an earthquake in

1303, the interior contains an anonymous Martyrdom of St Catherine (1389). Far more interesting is the little church of **Madonna dei Bagni**, by the side of the N3, just 2km south of Deruta. The walls of this church are covered in votive majolica tiles and they constitute, in themselves, both a miniature museum of majolica and a fascinating insight into everyday life, with all its hazards and tragedies, from the 17th century to the present day.

The custom of commissioning votive tiles to hang in the church dates back to 1657 when, according to local legend, a merchant called Cristoforo nailed a tile, painted with the image of the Virgin, to an oak tree. He prayed to the image, asking for his wife, who lay on her deathbed, to be cured. When he arrived home he found her fit and well. A church was built alongside the oak tree and from that time onwards local people have brought their tiles to the church in the hope of a similar miracle.

The tiles depict, in vivid colours, the whole range of human misfortunes, from accidents at home to fire and flood. The date range spans the age of the horse and the age of the motorcar. Unscrupulous thieves stole some of the earliest tiles in 1980 and the church is now more closely guarded. It is usually open in the morning, again after evening mass (18.00) and on Saturdays.

Todi

From Deruta the N3 speeds us south to Todi, a characteristic Umbrian hilltop town with the pointed tower of San Fortunato dominating the hilltop, and the domed bulk of Santa Maria della Consolazione competing for attention in the plain below.

Commanding the promontory between the valleys of the Tiber and the Naia, Todi has long had strategic importance and was settled as early as the 5th century BC. The town's ubiquitous coat of arms, featuring an eagle with a napkin in its talons, refers to the legend that Todi was founded on the spot where the eagle let the napkin drop, after it had seized it from an Etruscan banqueting table.

In the pre-Roman era the Tiber formed the boundary between Etruscan territory to the west and Umbrian territory to the east. Todi's Etruscan name – Tutare – means border and it is probable that the town was founded as a frontier fort. The people of the town have a reputation for defending their liberty with great ferocity; they turned Hannibal away (in recognition of which the town was given the honorary name Marzia after the Roman god of war) and they also refused to bow to the might of Totila the Goth.

Apart from three sets of walls – Etruscan, Roman and medieval – there is little reminder of those turbulent times in the appearance of the city today. Instead, it is a town of great beauty, blessed with views over unspoiled countryside. Its narrow streets are filled with flowers and many medieval houses have been restored to serve as weekend and holiday homes, principally for Romans.

From the car park near the Piazza Oberdan, close to Santa Maria della Consolazione, it is a short climb to **San Fortunato** at the highest point in the town. Fortunato was the appropriately named bishop who led Todi in its

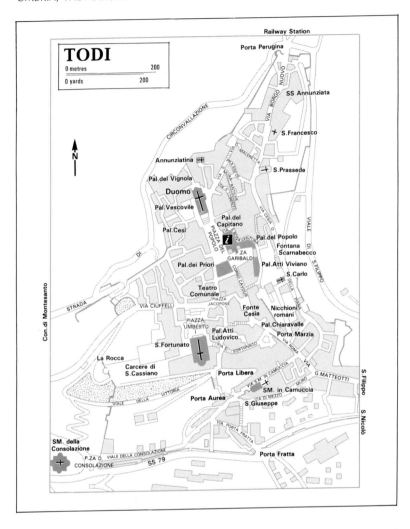

resistance to Totila, succeeding where his counterpart in Perugia, Bishop Herculanus, failed. Fortunato was made the patron saint of Todi in gratitude and this huge church was built in his honour, beginning in 1292.

The magnificent Gothic portal, set into the half-finished façade, was not added until 1436 – late for the Gothic style. Yet in no sense is this the work of backward masons out of touch with mainstream architectural trends; it is an exquisite work with delicate mouldings crowded with figures and vivid vignettes illustrating Biblical stories.

The huge echoing interior is, for once, not a disappointment. Sunlight pours in through the windows of the aisles, once blocked but now reopened. The

Todi's streets, with their carefully laid cobblestones, are a work of art in themselves

sense of lightness is reinforced by the height and slenderness of the composite columns, surrounded by clusters of shafts, rising up to massive Corinthian columns from which the roof vaults spring.

The aisles are almost as tall as the nave and a further unusual, and pleasing, feature is the running arcade separating the aisles from the side chapels. Recent restoration has involved shoring up the walls with timbers (painted grey) to arrest the subsidence which is a problem throughout Todi. The walls and ceilings have either been stripped to bare stone or painted white so that the few surviving frescoes shine out with intense colour. The best fresco, in the fourth chapel on the right, is Masolino da Panicale's delicate and dreamy *Madonna and Child* (1432).

The ornate choir stalls of the chapel are the work of Maffei da Gubbio (1590). The crypt contains a huge Baroque mausoleum to Saints Cassianus and Callixtus. A much more modest plaque marks the burial place of the Franciscan poet, Jacopone (1250–1306), the author of the *Stabat Mater Dolorosa*. He was also a zealous critic of Pope Boniface VIII and was imprisoned for five years towards the end of his life for leading a Franciscan revolt against church corruption. Perhaps that is why a man who is now regarded as one of the great early medieval poets, one of the first to write in Italian, was not honoured with a memorial until 1596.

San Fortunato stands alongside the town's public gardens, planted with cypress trees and box hedges, from which there are views of the wild hillsides that roll away into the distance to the west of Todi. To the left of the church a path leads down to Via San Fortunato and the Porta Marzia, the town's one surviving Etruscan gate. This straddles the Corso Cavour, the main street, which leads to the broad **Piazza del Popolo**.

This piazza is one of the most striking in all Umbria. Its beauty has, perhaps, been exaggerated; the buildings are robust rather than graceful, but the square has changed little in appearance since the end of the 14th century. The sense of being surrounded by medieval buildings, still used for their original purposes, is remarkable and to be paralleled only by one of England's great cathedral closes.

The medieval appearance is, to a degree, the result of restoration, which is still in progress. At the end of the piazza, the Palazzo dei Priori has been converted to serve as the town library with shops below. The building was begun in 1293 and completed in 1369 when the campanile was added. Its most striking feature is the great bronze eagle, the symbol of the town, cast in 1339 and positioned above the library entrance.

The two buildings on the right-hand side of the square (as you face the cathedral) are the Palazzo del Capitano, dating to 1292, fronted by a fine staircase, and the Palazzo del Populo, with its Ghibelline fishtail battlements, begun in 1213 and one of the oldest surviving public buildings in Italy.

All we can do for the present is admire the exteriors, especially the fine Gothic triple lancets of the Palazzo del Capitano. At some time in the future (and nobody is prepared to say when) the museum in this palazzo will reopen, providing an opportunity to see the collection inside, which contains outstanding Etruscan bronzes excavated from tombs in the Todi district, and Lo Spagna's *Coronation of the Virgin* (1507).

The **Duomo**, at the far end of the square, is another interesting building that incorporates Romanesque, Gothic and Renaissance classical features. The symmetrical façade, rising from a broad staircase, has three doorways and three intricate rose windows – the latter inserted in 1520. The central portal is surrounded by fine leafscroll carving and the wooden doorway, dating to the 17th century, is equally ornate.

Inside the nave arcades are typically Romanesque, with round arches rising from the columns, which are alternately square in section, with side shafts, and round. The square columns have capitals carved with Biblical scenes while the round columns, of green marble, seem almost too slender to support their massive Corinthian capitals, let alone the great expanse of wall that rises above. Together, these columns represent the massive and simple forms of the Romanesque and the more delicate forms of the Gothic, blended in an unusual way at a time when one style was being superseded by the other.

The Gothic is more fully realised in the splendid arcade that separates the south aisle from the side chapels, all slender shafts, pointed arches and rib vaulting.

The outstanding woodwork of the choir was made in 1530 by Antonio and Sebastiano Bencivenni. Each stall is decorated with intarsia work panels of great detail, some representing views into the interiors of rooms, as if seen through a window, others showing religious scenes, such as the Annunciation. Panels below the seats show the woodworker's tools used in making this intricate work.

The dark crypt descends into a part of the church that dates to pre-Roman times, for the cathedral is built on the site of an Etruscan temple. As you emerge and head for the exit you will notice that the entire west wall is painted with a *Last Judgement* fresco, the work of Ferraù da Faenza. It dates from the early 17th century and is a copy of Michelangelo's scenes in the Sistine Chapel, but is none the less striking.

From the cathedral steps it is well worth turning left and walking down the Via del Duomo, both to look at the external detail of the Romanesque apse and for the views from the little belvedere. This stands on the site of one of four gates at the corners of the Piazza del Popolo that allowed the whole square to be sealed off and defended in the event of an attack.

The church of **Santa Maria della Consolazione**, outside the city walls, evokes mixed reactions. From afar it is a pleasing building of elegant form, consisting of a dome-topped cubic nave and four tall polygonal apses off each face of the cube. The setting, in an expanse of green lawn, backed by wooded hills, lends it further charm. At this stage we might be tempted to agree with those who have dubbed it one of Italy's finest Renaissance buildings.

The church of Santa Maria della Consolazione, a Renaissance jewel on the outskirts of Todi

Closer to, disillusionment begins to set in. The church, of creamy yellow stone, lacks zest. Perhaps this is because so many architects were involved. The design has been attributed to Bramante, the architect of St Peter's in Rome, but although there are many resemblances between the two churches, there is no evidence that Bramante was actually involved. The basic design is now thought to be the work of Cola da Caprarola but, between 1508 when construction began and 1607 when it was completed, many others lent a hand. All aesthetic hopes are dashed when you finally enter the church. For all the bravado of the exterior, the inside is marred by huge and lifeless Baroque figures of the Apostles and a poor fresco of Our Lady of Consolations.

From Todi you have a choice of roads to Orvieto. The N448 is fast and scenic, particularly where it clings to the hillside above the southern shores of Lake Corbara, fed by the River Tiber. Alternatively, if you are prepared to take longer and drive most of the way in low gear, the N79 bis is a delightful road. It climbs through a varied landscape of bare rock, cut by deep ravines, of scrub and of woodland, presenting ever-changing vistas. At **Prodo** you pass the picturesque castle overlooking Lake Corbara and for most of the journey you will be alone with nature. Butterflies, jays and lizards will skip, swoop or scuttle across your path and wherever you stop to take in the views the only sound you will hear is the hum of myriad insects going about their business amongst the herbs and wildflowers.

The last view, as you approach the end of the journey, is the best. The steep walls of Orvieto rise out of the bare rock of the plateau on which the city sits, backed by vineyard-covered hills, the source of the region's well-known wines. The striking brown cliffs below the city walls represent the eroded remains of a volcanic plug and the region's volcanic soils are responsible for the crisp dryness of Orvieto wine. Erosion has been, and remains, a problem. Medieval planning laws forbade the building of any structure around the edge of the plateau, called the *rupe*. Considerable sums of money have been spent in recent years to stabilise the cliffs, subject to frequent landslips.

Orvieto

When you enter Orvieto you discover that it is not quite the serene place it looks in distant views. The busy city is marred by traffic and this again contributes to the problem of erosion, through the combined effect of vehicle weight and vibration on the soft underlying tufa. A grand scheme to make Orvieto completely traffic-free is being implemented. Visitors are expected to park in Orvieto Scala, the modern lower town. From there a funicular railway will carry you up to the Piazzale Cahen, at the eastern end of the city. From there you can walk to the Duomo, or take a minibus.

The Duomo

Orvieto cathedral is, without doubt, the finest of its period in Italy and stands at the southern edge of the city. What you see first is the beautiful grey-and-white banded **exterior walls**. After the rough and unfinished exteriors of so many Umbrian churches, the completeness and refinement of this cathedral comes as a pleasant surprise. From the foundations to the gables, white travertine and dove-grey tufa alternate in horizontal bands 23cm in depth. The pretty side chapels, running round the nave, each have delicate trefoil-headed blank arcading beneath their limpet-shell roofs.

Such refinement is not Umbrian in character. For parallels you have to look west, to Siena in Tuscany. In the 12th and 13th centuries, Orvieto was one of the most powerful cities in central Italy and controlled a vast territory that stretched as far as the coast, including Siena itself. Since Orvieto was westward-looking in its trade and politics, it was natural enough to call on Tuscan architects for assistance in building the cathedral.

The scheme to build a new cathedral was first mooted in 1264, a year after a miracle occurred at Bolsena. This little town, 21km south west of Orvieto, was visited by a priest from Bohemia, travelling to Rome in order to resolve his personal doubts over the truth of the doctrine of transubstantiation. Celebrating mass in the town, the host literally turned to flesh at the moment of consecration, and drops of blood spilled on to the altar cloth.

As a consequence Pope Urban IV instituted the feast of Corpus Christi and Orvieto was chosen to house the precious blood-stained cloth. Work did not start on the cathedral, however, until 1290, when Pope Nicolas IV laid the foundation stone.

The original design is attributed, without confirmatory evidence, to the Florentine architect, Arnolfo di Cambio, who had already been involved in the construction of the cathedral and the Palazzo Vecchio in his native city. He was assisted, perhaps, by Fra Bevignate, the friar who designed Perugia's Fontana Maggiore and Palazzo dei Priori.

Their work ground to a halt when the original scheme was compromised by attempts to graft elements of the newly fashionable Gothic style on to the Romanesque structure. A Sienese architect, Lorenzo Maitani, was brought in to resolve the constructional problems and, starting in 1310, he was responsible for the distinctive Sienese flavour of the building.

Maitani strengthened the nave with massive piers and buttresses so that the walls could take the Gothic stone vault. Some of these piers can be seen on the west façade – once you have had time to realise that the extraordinarily rich carving of this façade does in fact disguise four huge and bulky masonry columns.

The first point to notice is the clever marriage between Maitani's massive piers, forming an almost continuous wall of stone, and the delicate Gothic structure above, a confection of pink, white and green marble encrusted with mosaics and cosmati work. The bulk of the piers is such that the side portals are very narrow, by necessity squeezed into a constricted space. What

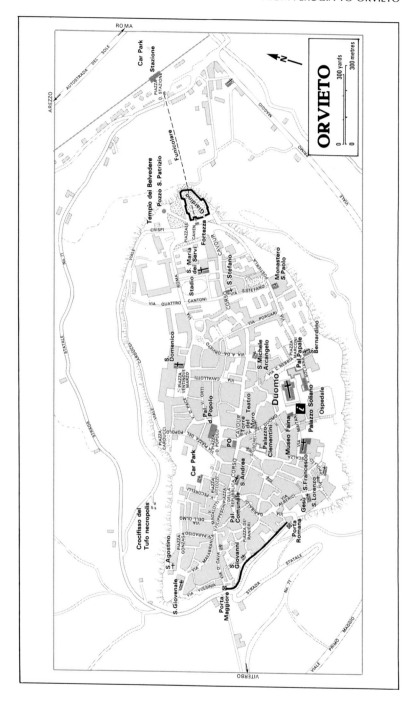

Orvieto's zebra-striped Duomo was built in Sienese style to celebrate the Miracle of Bolsena

prevents the lower façade looking ill-proportioned in relation to the rest is the wonderful sequence of bas reliefs that cover the surface of the rosy pink stone, distracting the eye from the mass of the structure.

Before looking at the carvings themselves, it is best to take in the rest of the façade, perhaps from the comfort of the stone benches on the opposite side of the piazza. Numerous artists worked on the cathedral after Maitani and progress was halting. The great wheel window was completed by about 1380, along with the mosaic figures in the spandrels, depicting the Four

Doctors of the Church, the sequence of fifty busts of saints set in quatrefoils in the surrounding frame (with Christ at top centre) and the side niches filled with figures of the prophets.

Antonio Frederighi took over in 1452 and he carved the animated figures of the Apostles that occupy the upper tier of niches. The triangular cusps, forming the central and side pediments, came last, added in 1619, some 355 years after the cathedral was first conceived. The mosaics which lend colour to the façade are nearly all 17th century or later. Earlier but restored works survive in the triangular cusps above the portals and depict (left to right) the *Baptism of Christ* (1584), the *Assumption* (1388) and the *Birth of the Virgin* (1364).

Moving up to the cathedral face, it is sad to discover that the wonderful bas reliefs are partly covered in perspex sheeting; even more distressing to learn the reason – these extraordinary sculptures were vandalised in 1982 – but cheering, at least, to see that swift and expert restoration has minimised the long-term damage.

Each pier follows essentially the same scheme; a central vine, with leaves and tendrils branching to the left and right, forms the framework for a series of vignettes; the first pier illustrates Genesis, the second the stories of Abraham and David, the next the life of Christ, and the fourth the Last Judgement.

Attributions are impossible to make; it is estimated that more than 150 sculptors contributed to these intricate and forceful narratives, including Maitani and his son, Vitale, and Andrea Pisano, the sculptor of Perugia's Fontana Maggiore.

Some vignettes are humorous – God delving into the side of Adam to draw out a rib to create Eve, for example, and Adam and Eve hiding from their creator in the bushes, having eaten the Forbidden Fruit. Some are charming: in the Nativity scene Mary lifts a blanket to gaze at her sleeping son while Joseph nods, exhausted and bewildered by the events that surround him, in the foreground. Some are arresting, most especially the dramatic Last Judgement scenes, where real human misery is written in the faces of the wretched souls who have discovered that their fate is to suffer eternal torment.

Some last details to note before entering the cathedral are the bronze symbols of the Evangelists, cast by the versatile Maitani, above each pier, the *baldacchino*, with angels by Maitani and a Madonna and Child by Andrea Pisano in the central lunette, and the bronze doors designed by Emilio Greco in 1963. Greco's work, once controversial for its modernity, depicts the Corporeal Works of Mercy.

After the sumptuous façade the cathedral **interior** is calm and serene. Pews, monuments and Baroque edifices have been swept away, leaving us with an uninterrupted view across the sun-dappled floor of ox-blood coloured marble. The sublime nave, Romanesque in conception and Gothic in details such as the pointed windows, is of the same banded grey and white stone as the exterior, with circular columns, fine bracketed capitals and a graceful clerestory. The whole is remarkably unified and betrays none of the difficulties that were encountered by the various architects who worked upon it.

Detail on the façade of Orvieto's Duomo showing the Nativity

The single splash of colour that you see from the nave is provided by the tall east window, filled with 14th-century stained glass. The frescoes to either side, by Ugolino, are enshrouded by scaffolding, as are the world-famous frescoes by Signorelli in the Cappella Nuova, off the right-hand transept. All we have to remind us of the force and imaginative scope of these great paintings is a small exhibition, with photographs, explaining the restoration process, which is likely to continue for a decade or more.

The photographs provide tantalising glimpses of an extraordinarily powerful vision of the Apocalypse. The gentle monk, Fra Angelico, of whom Henry James wrote, 'all his paintings convey a passionate pious tenderness', painted two scenes in this chapel in 1447. Fifty years then elapsed before Signorelli came along and surrounded Fra Angelico's lyrical work with appalling scenes of the Antichrist, the end of the world and the damned in Hell.

There is scarcely anything else in art quite like Signorelli's cycle – unless it is the Sistine Chapel ceiling, for Michelangelo was deeply impressed by Signorelli's stunning draughtsmanship and copied his brilliantly foreshortened perspective. The other parallel that springs spontaneously to mind, no matter how inappropriate it may seem, is modern sci-fi and fantasy art. Signorelli's metal-winged monsters and menacing green-faced devils seem to belong to the nightmare world of the heavy rock album cover. No-one else, though, has so brilliantly expressed a sense of the world coming to an end in a chaos of revolution and dissolution, with twisted bodies flying everywhere as if the law of gravity itself had suddenly ceased.

No photographs are provided to remind us of Ugolino's frescoes in the left-hand transept (also under restoration), which tell the story of the Miracle of Bolsena. It is, though, possible to see the bejewelled reliquary in which the Corporale, the blood-stained altar cloth, is housed, set within a huge tabernacle. The richly coloured frescoes that have been restored, either side of the tabernacle, are also by Ugolino, painted in 1364, and depict the Passion in dramatic detail.

West of the Duomo

The cathedral is Orvieto's highlight and, after seeing that, most visitors are content to do no more than wander up the Via dei Duomo to shop for majolica. If you want to do more, cross the pedestrianised Corso Cavour, the city's main shopping street, and go down Via della Constuenti to the Piazza del Popolo. This broad square, spoilt by its use as a car park, has a colourful morning street market. Across the square to the right is the Palazzo del Popolo, a striking 12th- and 13th-century building of intermediate Romanesque/Gothic style, built of pitted sandy brown tufa. Like so much in Orvieto, it is closed and under restoration.

If you return to Corso Cavour and turn right you will come to the church of **Sant' Andrea**, once an important church from which Pope Innocent III announced the Fifth Crusade in 1216, but since eclipsed by the cathedral. The crypt incorporates Etruscan and Roman masonry and the exterior has an elegant polygonal campanile and a loggia that now serves as a flower market.

Sant' Andrea looks down on the undistinguished Piazza della Repubblica and if you carry on a short distance west, down Via Malabranca, you will come to **San Giovenale**, Orvieto's first cathedral, perched on the edge of the plateau. Added on to the Romanesque nave, perhaps dating from the early 11th century, is a 13th-century Gothic sanctuary, the walls of which are covered in fragments of fresco, including a macabre Calendar of Funeral Anniversaries.

Alternatively you can head south from Sant' Andrea to the church of **San Lorenzo di Arari**. Arari means altar, and the cylindrical stone drum, set beneath the 12th-century stone canopy, is said to be an Etruscan sacrificial slab. Colourful and well-restored frescoes, dating to 1330, depict the life of St Lawrence, who seems not to mind the grilling he receives.

The Pozzo di San Patrizio

The last, and perhaps the best sight in Orvieto after the cathedral, lies back at the eastern edge of the city, off Piazzale Cahen. Here, alongside the public gardens that surround the remains of the 14th-century Fortezza and the ruins of an Etruscan temple, is a highly unusual artesian well, called the Pozzo di San Patrizio (St Patrick's Well – so called because of its supposed resemblance to a cave in which St Patrick dwelled in Ireland).

The well was dug in 1527 on the orders of Pope Clement VII who sought refuge in Orvieto after imperial troops had sacked Rome. Fearing a siege, Clement commissioned the local engineer, Antonio di Sangallo, to dig a shaft down through the soft tufa to tap the springs of St Zero below.

The shaft took ten years to sink and is 63m deep. An ingenious double spiral staircase, lit by openings in the well shaft, was constructed to allow pack horses to descend to collect water and ascend via a separate set of steps, thus avoiding collisions. Visitors can now follow the pack horse route, passing an Etruscan tomb that was discovered during excavation half way down the shaft, into the dark and chilly depths. The descent is difficult, and the ascent even more so, but for the energetic it is well worthwhile for the ever-changing vistas through the shaft openings and the strange subterranean lighting effects.

Practical Information

Tourist information offices

ORVIETO
Piazza del Duomo 24 (tel. 0763 41772).

TODI
Piazza del Popolo 38.

Where to stay

ORVIETO
Just 5km south of Orvieto, **La Badia** (La Badia 8, (tel. 075-90539)), converted from a 13th-century Benedictine monastery, has everything you could want: an outstanding rural setting, quiet cloisters, 13th-century frescoes, a swimming pool and an excellent restaurant (closed Jan and Feb).
Maitani, Via Maitani 5 (tel. 075-42011): Named after the cathedral architect, this hotel is converted from a 16th-century palazzo and is almost opposite the cathedral itself (closed 7–22 Jan).
Antico Zoppo, Via Marrabottini 2 (tel. 075-40370): Clean, attractive and reasonably priced.

Where to eat

ORVIETO
Il Molino, Via Garibaldi 41, (tel. 075-41952), is Orvieto's best and most expensive restaurant and a favourite with Hollywood film stars (closed Weds and 6–31 Jan).
Le Grotte del Funaro, Via Ripa Serancia 41 (tel. 075-43276): Sample Umbrian cooking in a series of caves cut into the tufa but surprisingly elegant (closed Mon).

Del Pino da Cecco, Via di Piazza del Popolo 15/21 (tel. 075-42661): Good value, adventurous cooking by a patroness who has been honoured for her culinary skills (closed Tues — except in summer — and Jan).

9. SOUTHERN UMBRIA

From Orvieto the N448 heads south east to the southern tip of Lake Corbara; it crosses the Tiber and the A1 autostrada and then, just before the road swings east to Todi, a right turn takes you to the quiet village of **Baschi**. There is nothing compelling here to stop for, just a peaceful square high above the Tiber valley and the 11th-century church of San Nicolò, with a 16th-century façade of buff-coloured stone.

Four kilometres south of Baschi, turn left away from the Tiber and follow a prettily winding road past the turn (after another 5km) to Montecchio. As you turn south towards Guardea, you will see Montecchio, rising high on the left, its houses gleaming white in the sunshine and, going through Guardea (5km down the road), you will catch sight of the man-made Lake Alviano, far below in the valley to the right.

Lugnano and Amelia

Finally you reach **Lugnano in Tevere**, located on one of the highest hills in this gently hilly region, 319m above sea level. The inhabitants of this sleepy town enjoy the most stupendous all-round views and at this distance the Tiber valley looks idyllic, its railway and autostrada lost in the haze.

The views are not the sole reason for stopping here. The highlight of this town is one of Umbria's finest and least-spoiled Romanesque churches, **Santa Maria Assunta** (Our Lady of the Assumption). The church is fronted by a 13th-century loggia with a great deal of interesting sculpture carved along the capitals and eaves course: symbols of the Evangelists, birds and human heads and a corbel table of beast heads. Most remarkable of all is a bearded figure carved on the left-hand wall; this represents the Trinity and shows three human faces – one face-on and two in profile on either side.

The upward-curving roof of the loggia meets the rough travertine façade of the 12th-century church. The same Four Evangelists are carved in the spandrels of the frame enclosing the wheel window. Above, a six-petalled flower (rosetta) is surrounded by seven plates of coloured majolica, representing the

Seven Sacraments. The eagle crowning the pediment is from the coat of arms of Pope Innocent III.

This ancient façade is neither pretty nor great architecture, but it is endearing and the most ornate building in the town – as if the local people had pulled out the stops to make this one building special. Sadly, much of the cosmati work has gone from its frames. The church would once have looked even more ornamental with its original mosaic patterns of green, red and gold.

Inside the loggia is an intriguing tablet dated 1 April 1230. It records an agreement, sworn by all the men of Lugnano, not to incur any debt on behalf of the community, on pain of a fine of 1000 silver marks. One wonders what embarrassing debt might have given rise to this joint resolution – perhaps the funds raised for the building of the loggia itself.

The interior of the church is considerably more sophisticated than the exterior, and is especially interesting by virtue of the survival of an almost complete set of 12th-century furnishings. The delightful inlaid marble floor was restored in 1969 by Paoloni Corrado who explained that the three marbles employed represent the Three Theological Virtues: white for Faith, green verde antico for Hope and red porphyry for Charity.

Four colums on either side separate the aisles from the nave and the third capital on the left is carved with a priest celebrating Communion. His right hand is raised in blessing in the manner of the Byzantine rite, with thumb and ring finger joined. The same capital is carved with a female figure, symbolising ecclesia, the church, holding the eucharist, and an owl and the moon, symbolising wisdom and vigilance.

The Byzantine gesture is tantalising, especially when you realise that the chancel and apse is furnished in the Greek manner, with a pair of marble amboes – pulpits for reading the Epistle and the Gospel, both beautifully decorated with cosmati work. Behind the amboes is a graceful marble screen, open at the top and with two bas relief panels below: on the left, two men in flowing, long-sleeved robes exchange the kiss of peace and, on the right, the Archangel Michael thrusts his spear into the mouth of a dragon.

The high altar is raised on a dais behind the marble screen. In the eastern Communion rite, curtains suspended from the screen would be drawn to hide the central mystery of the consecration of the host from the congregation. The existence of these ornate fittings suggests not that the eastern liturgy was practised in 12th-century Lugnano, but rather that the builders of this church must have had some knowledge of the Byzantine-inspired churches of Ravenna, on the Adriatic coast, which has similar furnishings. How these accomplished masons came to be employed to furnish an out-of-the-way church in Umbria is an intriguing mystery.

In the atmospheric crypt, among the slender columns and the walls built of massive blocks of travertine, there is an early 14th-century Crucifixion fresco and a sophisticated triptych by Niccolo Alunno, representing the Assumption of the Virgin, flanked by Saints Francis and Sebastian.

Amelia

Nearly 11km south east of here, **Amelia** is a town ringed by massive walls, built of great polygonal blocks of stone. Some are 2m or more across, interlocked with great skill and held together by the sheer weight of the masonry.

Great claims have been made for the antiquity of these defences. Pliny dates the foundation of the town to 1134BC and Cato thought Amelia one of the oldest settlements in Italy. In fact they probably date to the 5th century BC, which is ancient enough, and they have stood not only the ravages of Totila the Goth but also several earthquakes that have shaken the town, the latest serious one occurring in 1812.

Tiny gateways pierce the walls, leading to a town of steep cobbled streets and stone staircases, a place in which to wander and lose yourself, spotting fragments of Roman masonry incorporated into the façades of medieval houses.

The fire and earthquake-damaged churches do not, at first, look especially interesting, but the church of Santi Filippo e Giacomo, in Piazza Augustus Vera, has an elegant 15th-century cloister and a series of tombs, dating to the same century, carved with bas reliefs by Agostino di Duccio, belonging to the local Geraldini family.

The ugliness of the cathedral, at the highest point in the town, is mitigated by another tomb to Bishop Geraldini, also by Duccio, carved with a delicate Virgin and Child and the Four Cardinal Virtues. Two Turkish flags in the right-hand chapel were taken at the Battle of Lepanto.

Narni and Carsulae

Journeying east, your heart may sink as you leave behind the unspoilt Umbrian countryside and approach Narni with its smoke stacks and steel works; but Narni itself remains aloof from its industrial offspring, Narni Scalo, and little of the disfiguring sprawl in the valley can be seen from the hilltop town.

Narni

Narni stands high on a promontory above the River Nera. It is the southernmost of the Umbrian hilltowns, for beyond lies the flatter region of Lazio. Industry has, at least, brought new prosperity to Narni, for the town was in decline until the 1950s and for that reason many of the buildings still have a slightly dilapidated appearance.

The **cathedral** stands broadside on to the wide Piazza Garibaldi and is dedicated to the town's first bishop and patron saint, Juvenalis. A delightful 15th-century Renaissance portico fronts the church, but inside all is Roman-esque. The nave arcade has unusually flat arches, above which fragments of 12th-century frescoes have survived.

The Porta Ternana, the ancient gateway guarding the entrance to Narni

Narni's ancient heart, the **Piazza dei Priori**, lies to the left of the cathedral as you emerge, scarcely wide enough to deserve the name piazza. The twenty-sided fountain in the centre bears some resemblance to Perugia's Fontana Maggiore and dates to 1303.

The **Palazzo dei Priori**, on the right, was designed by Gattapone; the palazzo consists of a tall white campanile with an external pulpit and a massive loggia, supported by a central octagonal column, which now serves as a covered market.

Opposite, the **Palazzo del Podestà** is clearly made up of three separate structures, including the stump of a 13th-century defensive tower. Unity is provided by six fine mullioned and transomed windows on the upper floor, dating to the 15th century.

An intriguing set of sculptured panels is set into the palace façade to the right of the main door. They are very similar in style to the panels on the façade of San Pietro in Spoleto and, if they are by the same hand, could date to the late 12th century. They depict a beheading, a lion and a griffin, two figures on horseback, one with a hawk, and two jousting knights.

Clearly these reliefs were not made especially for the palace, but the jousting scene at least is appropriate. In May, on the feast of St Juvenalis, the town celebrates the Festa dell' Anello, the Festival of the Ring, when horsemen in knightly costume compete to thrust a lance through a metal hoop. The festival recalls the fact that Narni was once famous for the bravery of its soldiers, notably the mercenary Erasmo di Narni (nicknamed 'Gattamelata' – the honey cat) who was honoured by the Republic of Venice and whose equestrian statue by Donatello can be seen in Padua.

The council chamber, or Sala del Consiglio, on the first floor of the palazzo houses an outstanding painting, Ghirlandaio's *Coronation of the Virgin* (1486), as well as Lo Spagna's fresco of St Francis receiving the stigmata.

Further down, past the fountain, at the head of Via Mazzini, you will find the modest but charming church of Santa Maria delle Pensole. An inscription above the figure of Christ in Majesty on the façade dates the church to 1175. A beautiful frieze of vine scroll frames the portals. Two caryatids support the ends of the frieze and the central portal is flanked by lions devouring sacrificial lambs. The same flattened arches of tufa appear here as we saw in the cathedral, supported on great pillars most of which have Corinthian capitals – though one is carved with two lions devouring a man.

As you emerge from the church, note the pleasing window surrounds of the Renaissance palazzo opposite, carved with scallop shells. Further down Via Mazzini, the **art gallery** housed in the church of San Domenico (open 8.00–14.00) contains Benozzo Gozzoli's excellent *Annunciation*.

At the opposite end of town, the narrow Via del Monte leads off the Piazza Garibaldi and climbs up through the medieval quarter – strictly the medieval third since Narni was divided into three districts, this one called the Terziere di Mezule. The **Rocca Albornoz**, a papal castle built in the 1370s, stands at the top of the hill, from which there are fine views over the valley of the River Nera.

Narni's long and narrow main square, the Piazza dei Priori

This narrow valley is spanned by the single remaining arch of a Roman bridge, the **Ponte d'Augusto**, which carried the Via Flaminia over the Nera. Town guides make much of this fragment but it is not really worth the walk. Instead, look out for the bridge as you leave the town on the N3, heading north towards Todi. As you cross the modern bridge, before you enter the tunnel, look right and you will see the arch at the same height as the modern road.

The N3 northwards quickly narrows to a scenic lane winding through prosperous villa and vineyard country to San Gémini. Two kilometres beyond this village, take the right turn to San Gémini Fonte – look for the Ristorante Carsulae on the right – and then the rough track on the left that leads you into the heart of Carsulae. Suddenly, all modern Umbria is left behind and you find yourself on top of a plateau surrounded by the walls and buildings of an ancient Roman town.

Carsulae

Founded around 220BC, and built either side of the Via Flaminia, Carsulae blossomed briefly but was hit by an earthquake towards the end of the 1st century AD. Never rebuilt, the masonry was stolen and weeds gradually hid the remains. The ancient town was rediscovered again in the 16th century and excavations have continued sporadically ever since.

The only roofed structure on the site is the 11th-century chapel of San Damiano, built of brick, tile and stone from the forum and fronted by a portico supported on Roman pillars. Just in front of the church, the original Via Flaminia climbs up through the centre of the town, its stone-paved surface rutted with wheel grooves. Following the road northwards, you pass two temples on the left. Their walls retain some original marble cladding and the delicate pink colour of the stone hints at the lost splendour of this town described as beautiful by Tacitus and Pliny.

The forum comes next, and the law courts, followed by an expanse of unexcavated sheep pasture. To the right, in the distance, you can see the little village of Portaria clinging to the steep sides of the Naia valley. Finally you reach the northern gate of the town, and the cemetery with two large intact and circular funerary monuments.

On the left-hand side of the Via Flaminia, as you return, are the baths and cisterns. The amphitheatre, built into the sides of a large natural hollow, is the most complete building on the site, and stands side by side with the theatre. From here you can look back to the one surviving arch of the temple, across a grassy plain littered with the fallen columns and white masonry of this once impressive colony.

From Carsulae, take the rough track that forks right (south), instead of returning along the track by which you arrived; this takes you to **Cesi**, known as the 'Belvedere' because of its position on a ledge against the side of Monte Torre Maggiore, and the extensive views over the Nera valley. Stones from Carsulae were used to build some of the churches of this attractive little town as well as, perhaps, the castle, built in 1323 but now itself in ruins.

If you have the time, you can climb or drive to the 12th-century church of **Sant' Erasmo**, 790m up the mountainside and close to an astronomical observatory, or to the summit of Monte Torre Maggiore itself (1121m) for even more extensive views.

With memories of the wonderful natural scenery in your mind, you descend towards the nondescript suburbs of Terni through acres of olive groves, thriving on the sunny south-facing slopes of the mountain.

Practical Information

Tourist information office

NARNI
Piazza dei Priori 12

Where to stay

NARNI
Dei Priori, Vicolo del Commune 4 (tel. 0744-726 843). Small and comfortable, in a medieval palazzo down a quiet lane.

Where to eat

NARNI
La Loggia, Vicolo del Commune 4 (tel. 0744-722 744). The restaurant of the Hotel dei Priori, sought out by gourmets for its remarkably inexpensive and adventurous food (closed Mon and last two weeks of July).

10. TERNI AND THE VALNERINA

Terni

Terni is like no other city in Umbria. It is the industrial capital of the region and, with a population of over 110,000, it is also the largest city. Terni usually receives a bad press from travel writers who perhaps forget that the city was almost totally destroyed during World War II. The city's modern appearance is therefore the result of rapid post-war reconstruction, not the result of wilful insensitivity to the medieval heritage.

Having said that, Terni has long been an industrial city – indeed the Industrial Revolution in peninsular Italy began here and Terni was known as the 'Italian Manchester' in the late 19th century. Terni built Italy's first steelworks, tapped the fast-flowing waters of the River Velino to generate hydro-electric power, began producing plastics as early as the 1920s, and has long been the centre of the Italian armaments industry – one dubious claim to fame is that the rifle used to assassinate President Kennedy was manufactured here.

Despite all this Terni still has some attractions. The 20 per cent of the city that escaped destruction during the Allied air raids of 1943–1944 is concentrated around the cathedral, conveniently reached by parking in the Corso del Popolo in the southern part of the city. From here it is a short walk to the public gardens that surround the Duomo. The gardens are bounded by a substantial stretch of Roman wall and include the remains of the Roman amphitheatre, built in AD32.

Following the main path through the gardens you emerge on to Via Cavour, a street lined with Renaissance palaces, now used by academic institutions and local government. Via Cavour leads into the vast central piazza – not one square but two; the Piazza Europa to the right is dominated by the vast and forbidding Palazzo Spada (1546) and the Piazza della Repubblica to the left is surrounded by functional 1950s public buildings.

The aim is to negotiate the latter square without being run over, and to reach the **Pinacoteca** on the far side, located behind the post office in Via Fratini and housed in the 17th-century Palazzo Manassei (open 9.00–14.00, closed Mon). The collection includes Benozzo Gozzoli's *Marriage of St Catherine* and a gonfalone from Siena invoking God's protection from plague. As befits a modern city there are several more recent works by Miró, Kandinsky, Chagall and Leger, but the most interesting pictures are those of the naïve artist and shoemaker, Orneore Metelli (1872–1938). He is the L. S. Lowry of Terni in the sense that he painted local industrial landscapes – steelworks rendered in vivid colour – as well as contemporary events, such as Mussolini's motorcade passing through the city.

Back in the main square turn left and left again, almost opposite the Palazzo Spada, to find the church of **San Salvatore**, the real reason for coming to Terni. This tiny and delightful church, standing in a garden, seems out of time and out of place amongst the surrounding apartment blocks.

The striking feature of San Salvatore is its circular sanctuary or rotunda which, inside, resembles a beehive: the dome, built of travertine, is elongated and rises to a circular porthole at the apex, positioned directly above the altar. Although of uncertain date, it is generally agreed that the rotunda was built as a temple to the sun, perhaps by the Umbrians as early as the 3rd century BC. It was then incorporated into a Roman house which perhaps served as a meeting place for early Christians in the 5th century. The nave was added in the 12th century and the little Cappella Manessei, to the left of the nave, was added in the 14th century. Numerous 13th- and 15th-century frescoes decorate the walls. Simple but beautiful, San Salvatore is a touching and surprising survival in this modern city.

If you cross back to the Palazzo Spada, turn left down Via Roma and right down Via Aminale, you will reach the front of the **Duomo**. Baroque and lacking in charm, the portico nevertheless hides two fine portals: the central one, Romanesque in style and carved with acanthus leaf trails inhabited by birds and beasts, and an equally fine Gothic one on the right, carved with foliage.

The 16th-century **Palazzo Bianchini-Riccardi**, opposite, is being restored. The beautiful entablature of the eaves course makes this Terni's most elegant building.

Another claim to world fame which Terni confidently asserts is that St Valentine is buried here. The Basilica di San Valentino is in the suburb of San Valentino, 2km south of the city centre. The head of the mummified saint was stolen in 1986 but his body remains and the town honours Valentine with a festival on 14 February.

Other Italian cities also claim to have the relics of the patron saint of lovers. Early martyrologies record two St Valentines – a Roman priest who died in AD269 and is now buried in the church of St Praxedes in Rome, and this one, the Bishop of Terni, who died in AD273. The Roman one is more usually associated with lovers, but the problem is further complicated by the existence of another Valentine, Bishop of Genoa. Chaucer, in his love poetry, frequently refers to 2 May – the feast of the Genoese saint – as St Valentine's Day.

The Valnerina

The landscape of Umbria, always varied, changes dramatically as you leave Terni. Ironically, the most industrialised city stands alongside one of the most beautiful rivers in Italy, and the valley of the River Nera, the Valnerina, remains wild, dramatic and little visited, with the exception of the Marmore Falls to the east of the city.

The Marmore Falls

The Cascata delle Marmore is a stupendous man-made waterfall some 162m in height. The fall was engineered under the rule of the Roman consul Curius Dentatus in 271BC. Surrounded by rivers, the plains around Terni were constantly subject to flooding, and always marshy. The Romans diverted the River Velino away from the plain in order to drain it. They cut a channel to carry the Velino northwards where it joins the River Nera. The slight waterfall that already existed, where the Nera spills over the side of Mount Marmore, became a powerful cascade with the combined force of the two rivers.

More recently, in 1938, the Velino was dammed at Lake Piediluco and the waters used to drive hydro-electric turbines. Consequently, the Marmore Falls dry to a mere trickle for much of the time. At certain times, though, the sluice gates are opened and the pent-up torrent comes pouring over the mountainside to crash thunderously down to the rocks below, sending up a mass of spray in which multiple rainbows quiver in the sunshine.

The waters are released according to a complicated timetable: from 15 July to 31 August you can see them any weekday, 17.00–18.30; on Saturdays, they operate March–April 18.00–21.00, May–August 17.00–21.00, September–October 18.00–21.00; on Sundays, November–March 15.00–16.00, April–August 10.00–12.00 and 15.00–21.00, and September–October 10.00–12.00 and 15.00–21.00.

If your first encounter with the falls whets your appetite to see them again, go at night when they are illuminated. You also have a choice of two viewpoints. The N209 out of Terni takes you to the base of the falls whereas the N79 takes you to the 'Belvedere Cascata' in the village of Marmore. From here you can walk alongside the river channel and past the sluice that controls the water flow, down to the belvedere itself, a look-out point dramatically suspended above the falls and with a spectacular view of the force.

Piediluco

If you take the N79 route you should carry on to the town of Piediluco alongside the lake of the same name. The town is ringed by mountains and distinctly alpine in appearance. The lake is a popular summer resort and hosts international rowing races as well as the water carnival, the Feste delle Acque.

Monte Caperno rises steeply to the south side of the lake and is reached

The man-made Cascata delle Marmore waterfall near Terni

by taking the station road, before you reach Piediluco itself. The mountain is famous for its echo which returns the sound of a shout perfectly after a four-second delay.

From Piediluco the road north to Arrone (12km) climbs steeply, with many a backward view of the lake, before crossing the watershed and descending into the narrow Valnerina. This wild and fascinating region, which includes a huge area of protected upland, designated a 'Parco Naturale Regionale', is still home to wolves and wild boar, not to mention a complex system of caves and potholes, mountain torrents, impenetrable ilex woods and flower-filled sheep pastures.

Ancient towers and crumbling fortresses dot the landscape, a legacy of the time when papal and imperial forces fought each other for territorial power in Umbria. Something of the rough, tough nature of the Valnerina in times past can be glimpsed at Ferentillo, one of the first villages you come to heading north along the N209 from Arrone. The curtain walls of this ancient citadel climb the steep hillsides either side of the gorge, dotted with look-out towers. No army or lone traveller could pass this way without being funnelled through the village and challenged. It is not surprising that this region remained a last stronghold of the Emperor, so well is the gorge defended.

Two soldiers from Napoleon's army who lost their way were seized here and summarily hanged. Their mummified remains are stored in the crypt of San Stefano, in that part of the village that stands on the right-hand side of the road. They are partnered by the remains of a Chinese couple who, by some bizarre circumstance, died here of cholera in the 19th century. These eerie corpses, like props from a horror movie, are the village's pride and joy, preserved by the dessicating effects of the biting winds that cut through the valley in winter.

San Pietro in Valle

A happier scene awaits just a couple of kilometres north. Here a cypress-lined avenue, to the left of the N209, climbs to the serene abbey of San Pietro in Valle. Part of the abbey is now privately owned and run as a restaurant, so by stopping here you can combine several pleasures.

Nobody knows for how long this broad shelf resting on the side of Mount Fironchi has been inhabited. Some have suggested that it is the site of the first legendary city of the Umbrians – Umbriano. With more certainty it is known that a monastery was established here early in the 8th century by the Lombardic Duke of Spoleto, Faroaldo II.

The Lombards, who invaded Italy in the wake of the Goths in the early 6th century, remained a powerful force in Umbria and the Marches for several centuries. They arrived as Teutonic pagans but settled and adopted Christianity – inspired by the example of St Benedict, born a mere 24km from here, in Norcia, and his Benedictine order of monks. When Faroaldo II was deposed in AD720 by his son, Trasamondo II, he decided to join the Benedictines and founded this monastery.

Much of the abbey complex, including the noble campanile, dates from the 12th century, but there are some earlier remains. The peaceful small cloister, to the right of the abbey church, incorporates sculptural fragments from Faroaldo's original building. The apse of the 8th-century church still stands and the extraordinary altar, carved with totemic figures and crude foliage, is inscribed with the name 'Ursus', the sculptor, and 'Iderico', who became Duke of Spoleto in AD739. Several very fine 3rd-century Roman sarcophagi are displayed here too and one of them, carved with Bacchic scenes, is supposed to have been used as Faroaldo's tomb.

Of equal interest are the frescoes of the nave, dating from the 1190s. Interspersed among later School of Giotto frescoes, they illustrate the *Creation* and *Adam and Eve in the Garden of Eden* (left), the *Nativity* and the *Crucifixion* (right). Few frescoes of this date survive in such good condition. Art historians regard them as among the first examples of an emerging Italian – as distinct from Byzantine – artistic style.

The mountain road to Cascia

Continuing up the N209, more fortifications rise from the valley sides – notably at **Scheggino** and **Vallo di Nera**. Scheggino is also the home of the Urbani family and headquarters of their truffle empire. This firm, it is estimated, is responsible for the collection and processing of 80 per cent of the truffle products consumed in Italy and 40 per cent of the world market.

Between Scheggino and Vallo di Nera, a road off the N209 heads east through Sant' Anatolia. This spectacular mountain road then passes through Monteleone and Cascia. After climbing steeply for several kilometres you reach high pastures where shepherds on horesback tend their flocks with the help of white-haired mountain dogs. Occasionally, too, you may see small herds of Umbria's famed white cattle, still bred here as draught animals since the hillside fields are often too steep for tractors.

Monteleone is the only town for several miles around, but remoteness does not, in this case, mean lack of prosperity. Newly built houses cluster around the old centre, paid for by the income from truffles and tourism. A few ancient masonry fragments and millstones are scattered across the green in front of the church of San Francesco and the portal has an endearing Gothic frame carved with lions, the symbol of the town, and the solitary figure of St Francis. The interior has pleasing 15th-century frescoes, including a homely Virgin suckling her child. A number of other artistic treasures from the church are now in New York's Metropolitan Museum.

Long before you reach **Cascia**, roadside signs advertising the Delle Rose Hotel announce that you are approaching an important pilgrim town. The hotel itself is one of the first buildings you see on arriving, for it is huge and unmissable, built in a commanding position overlooking the town. The hotel, painted pink, is a modern building, like so many in the town, for an earthquake in 1730 destroyed most of the ancient buildings.

The pilgrims – mainly women – come to pray at the shrine of St Rita, patron saint against infertility, of parenthood and of those in desperate situations. The latter covers a multitude of sad afflictions and disappointments which St Rita suffered in her own life. She was born in 1381 and wanted to become a nun; instead, she was forced to marry a man who was renowned for his infidelity and abused her for 18 years. Her two sons took after their father and when he was carried home dead one day, after a drunken brawl, they swore to seek revenge. Rita prayed that they should die rather than commit the mortal sin of murder – which they duly did a few days later of fever, but not before Rita had persuaded them to repent of their wicked lives.

Now childless and a widow, Rita sought the religious life for which she yearned. Three times she tried to enter Cascia's Augustinian convent and three times she was rejected on the grounds that the order would admit only virgins. Finally the Augustinian rule was amended on her behalf to permit widows to become nuns, and Rita entered the convent in 1413. In 1441, after years of self-imposed rigour, Rita received a form of the stigmata – a wound opened on her forehead as if it had been pierced by a crown of thorns. She died in 1457 and her body has remained 'uncorrupted' to this day. Pilgrims began to seek her out within years of her death because of the miracles attributed to her intervention, but she was not officially canonised until 1900.

The basilica that houses her shrine is a modern building, dated 1943 on the façade but not completed until 1947. The façade is its most interesting feature, built of polished travertine and in a modern version of Romanesque. Ten scenes from the life of the saint are carved in bold relief either side of the portal.

The interior is rather garishly coloured with modern frescoes and stained glass. The frescoes above the high altar illustrate another miracle that occurred in Cascia in 1330; a priest, called to give the last rites to a dying man, placed a consecrated host between the pages of his prayer book for safe carriage. On arrival at the sick man's house the pages of the book were found to be stained with blood. One of the pages is housed in a reliquary and brought out for veneration at the feast of Corpus Christi.

The mummified body of St Rita is housed in a glass casket in the gilded sanctuary to the left of the church. The walls are covered in tokens – principally silver hearts – donated by pilgrims. Stout Umbrian women come here to pray, confiding who knows what troubles to the silent saint.

If the idea of a modern pilgrimage town holds no appeal, you may still want to seek out some of the scenic hamlets around Cascia. Five kilometres to the west of the town, **Roccaporena** is a pretty hamlet in a magnificent setting beneath limestone crags with extensive views. St Rita was born here and married in the 13th-century church of San Martano. Nearby, Capanne di Collegiacone is a good departure point for mountain walks, following the footpaths that thread the pastures surrounding the hamlet.

Otherwise, speed on through Cascia to the junction of the N320 and N396 at Serravalle, and turn right on the fast level road that follows the pretty River Sardo into Norcia.

Practical Information

Tourist information offices

TERNI
Viale C. Battista 5 (tel. 0744 43047).

CASCIA
Piazza Garibaldi I (tel. 0743 71147).

Where to stay

TERNI
Garden Hotel, Via Bramante 6 (tel. 0744-43846). A pretty hotel with a small terraced garden and plant-filled balconies and a swimming pool.

PIEDILUCO
Casalago (tel. 0744-68421). The town's main hotel with fine gardens and lake views.

Where to eat

TERNI
Ludovico Tre Colonne, Via Plebiscito 13 (tel. 0744-54511). Relatively new but already noted for its excellent River Nera trout and local cheeses (closed Mon).
Da Carlino, Via Piemonte 1 (tel. 0744-420163). Out of the city centre with a beautiful garden and serving inexpensive local food (closed Mon and August).

ARRONE
Grottino del Nera (tel. 0744-78104). A simple and inexpensive trattoria by the side of the River Nera renowned for river trout, freshwater crayfish and truffle dishes (closed Wed and 10–24 Jan and 7–21 June).

11. NORCIA AND THE MARCHES

Norcia

It would be quite possible to visit Norcia without realising that this small town was the birthplace of St Benedict, the founder of western monasticism and a man who has been described as one of the architects of modern Europe. When Pope Paul VI proclaimed St Benedict patron saint of Europe in 1964, he said that monks, following the Benedictine rule of work and prayer (Ora et Labora), had colonised the outermost wilds of the continent, spreading civilisation from the Mediterranean to Scandinavia, from Ireland to Poland.

Whereas Assisi honoured St Francis with one of the greatest medieval churches in Christendom, Norcia has no more than a second-rate statue of St Benedict in its main square. The town is far more preoccupied with its reputation as a centre for the processing and curing of pork. The Piazza San Benedetto is ringed by *norcineria*, butchers' shops selling locally produced prosciutto, and numerous varieties of salami, ranging from tiny sausages to great meat-filled balloons.

The Norcians claim to have invented salami and there may be some truth in this, since sausagemakers all over Italy are called *norcini*. More contentiously, the town also claims that the word nursino, nurse, pays tribute to the medical skills of Norcia's Roman and medieval inhabitants. The same skills, perhaps, that make them good butchers seem to have been applied to the human body as well; not always, however, in the kindest manner, for Norcians once specialised in the castration of young male singers to provide a supply of castrato voices.

The modern appearance of Norcia owes much to the regular occurrence of earthquakes. Houses were deliberately built low (after the destructive tremor of 1859 an edict was issued setting a maximum height of 12.5m). Many buildings are still being reconstructed after the most recent violent earthquake which occurred in 1979.

Not a few buildings, especially in the north-eastern quarter of the town, were simply abandoned after the tremor. Now, though, the streets reverberate to the sound of demolition hammers and concrete mixers as the interiors are gutted and rebuilt. The reason is Norcia's latest phase of development as a ski resort: in a good year, the snows on the surrounding mountains remain until June (Virgil called the town 'frigida Nursia' – icy Norcia), although the mild winters of recent years have left many hotel owners wondering whether or not to shut up shop.

The centre of Norcia has a certain rough charm. The church of **San Benedetto** has an elegant Gothic portal and the upper portion of the façade a pretty geometric window, added when the church was rebuilt after the 1859 earthquake. The interior is sombre and uninviting but the crypt is worth exploring. It is built up against the foundations of the main temple of the Roman forum, and on the spot where St Benedict is supposed to have been born in AD480.

The altarpiece in the church, painted by Filippo Napoletano, dates to 1621 and illustrates St Benedict and Totila the Goth. The meeting between the two greatest men of their age, poles apart in their values, occurred in AD542, towards the end of the lives of both men.

Benedict, who had spent thirty years as abbot of the first monastic community at Subiaco, had now all but retired to his second foundation, Monte Cassino. Totila, who was making a triumphal progress through central Italy, laid waste by his armies, had heard of Benedict and decided to test his prophetic powers. According to the account given by Pope Gregory in his *Dialogues*, Totila sent Riggo, the captain of his guard, dressed in purple robes, to impersonate him. Benedict greeted Riggo with the words 'Put off those robes, my son, for they do not belong to you.'

Totila himself then came to see Benedict and prostrated himself before the great saint. They later spent some time in conversation, during which Benedict tried to persuade Totila to abandon his destructive onslaught. The meeting ended with Benedict's prophecy that Totila would succeed in sacking Rome but would die within ten years and not enjoy his conquest – a prediction that indeed came true.

Apart from this one painting, there is nothing else here to remind us of St Benedict or his contribution to western civilisation. Next to the church, the pleasing pink-stoned **Palazzo Communale**, raised above a delicate four-arched loggia, dates in part from the 14th century. Opposite, the squat **Castellina**, built in 1554 as a papal stronghold, contains a small museum (open 10.00–12.30, 14.00–17.00, closed Mon) with some rare 13th-century wooden figures of saints.

The town's most appealing building by far is the extraordinary **Edicola** (also known as the Tempietto, or little temple) on the corner of Via Umberto in the north of the town. This low tower, built in the mid 14th century, is covered in inscriptions and tiny but very detailed bas reliefs of masonic tools, the sun, Christ the Lamb and the instruments of the Passion, as well as very complex geometrical patterns and a corbel table of animal heads. No one quite knows what purpose this building served, but it may have been associated with a trade guild.

To the north of this building, the narrow streets and low houses of the Quartiere Capolaterra, the shepherds' quarter, is in the process of redevelopment, no doubt to provide weekend and winter homes for wealthy skiers.

Norcia's Piazza San Benedetto, named after St Benedict, founder of Western monasticism, who was born in the town

Here and there, though, you can still see ancient and crumbling houses where as much space was given to the winter quarters of sheep as to human habitation.

Due south of Norcia, a dead straight road passes through the town's industrial estate and leads to the hamlet of Santa Scolastica, named after the twin sister of St Benedict, about whom virtually nothing is known. Take the left turn in the hamlet, signposted to Castelluccio. Despite appearances on the map, this is a good, wide and relatively straight road that climbs rapidly to a height of over 1500m. As you begin the ascent the fertile plains south of Norcia are spread out to the right, irrigated by warm water springs that enable crops to be grown even in such an elevated and frequently cold situation.

Next, down on the left, Norcia itself is revealed far away below, nestling into the side of a natural amphitheatre at the foot of the Sibillini mountain range – so called because one of the highest peaks, Monte Vettore (2476m), was believed to be the home of a prophetic Sibyl.

Where the road divides at the summit of the pass, take the left turn. Here the landscape changes completely: no more trees and nothing but bare rounded hills and rocks. Finally, and dramatically, you pass over the rim of Mount Ventosola and see the vast Piano Grande spread out before you.

The Piano Grande and the Monti Sibillini

The Piano Grande (literally Great Plain) is the largest of three natural basins surrounding Castelluccio, the lone village just visible in the distance. The empty plain, 8km in length, is as flat as a cricket pitch, and virtually empty except for the odd haystack and field hut. If you come in winter the plain is bleak and dangerous to cross on foot – on the worst days bells are rung continuously in Castelluccio to guide inhabitants home. In early summer, by contrast, the grassland of the plain is one continuous flower meadow and later in summer, during the holiday season, the air is filled with hang-gliders who launch themselves from the rim of the surrounding mountains and coast down to the plain.

The sight may be familiar, too, if you have seen Zefferelli's film *Brother Sun, Sister Moon*, for much of it was shot here. Tiny **Castelluccio** itself is a scruffy working village that seems uncertain whether it wants the attention of tourists and sporting enthusiasts. The village, with a population of well under a hundred people, still lives by agriculture; Castelluccians crop hay from the plain to feed their cows, and grow tiny sweet lentils for which the area is famous all over Italy. A couple of makeshift bars have been created using battered caravans and scraps of corrugated iron to cater for the skiers and walkers who come here in increasing numbers and if you stop for coffee, fierce sheep dogs will bark at you and chickens, scrabbling among the manure heaps piled in the streets, stop for a while to look quizzically in your direction.

The village of Castelluccio sits on the rim of the Piano Grande beneath the high plateaux of the Monti Sibillini range

Castelluccio is, however, a perfect base for walking, surrounded as it is by a landscape of great natural beauty and interest. Immediately to the east, **Monte Vettore** rises to 2476m but the climb is not especially difficult in good weather if you are fit and well equipped, and will reward anyone interested in alpine flora.

To the south, around San Pellegrino, is the winter sports resort of **Forca Canapine**, right on the border of Umbria, the Marches and Abruzzo, with distant views to the Gran Sasso range, to the south east, peninsular Italy's highest group of mountains, rising to 2655m. A major roadbuilding programme currently under way will eventually link this resort to the Adriatic and Rome, so the air of peace and remoteness may not survive for long.

Part of the road is already finished, the stretch from Pescara (16km east of San Pelegrino) to the N4, and if you are staying in Castelluccio you can take the N4 – a spectacular highway of tunnels and elevated causeways – to visit **Ascoli Piceno** in the Marches. If you do visit Ascoli, be prepared for congested streets and a parking nightmare, but you might consider the trouble compensated by the city's outstandingly beautiful Piazza del Popolo, the works of art hung in the splendid Palazzo Communale and the Roman mosaics and sculptures in the Archaeological Museum.

The road north of Castelluccio crosses the unmarked border between Umbria and the Marches after a mile and then winds gently down through mountain scenery, dotted with ski-chalets, to meet the infant River Nera, finally to enter the little town of **Visso**. Visso sits in a hollow where five valleys meet and this

The elegant arcaded main square in Ascoli Piceno

picturesque setting rescues the town, a popular resort, from dullness. The houses may be modern but, wherever you look up you see changing vistas of wooded peaks and high pastures. All the interesting buildings are located around the central Piazza Martiri Vissani, with its 15th- and 16th-century palazzi and the collegiate church of Santa Maria, graced by a Romanesque portal and 15th-century frescoes.

As you head northwards to **Camerino**, the mountain landscape gradually gives way to the gentler hills that are typical of the Marches, a region that gained its name (*Marche* in Italian, from the German *mark*, meaning border or frontier) as early as the 10th century. The belt of countryside between Camerino and Fano, on the Adriatic coast, then served as a buffer zone marking the southern limits of lands controlled by the Lombards and later the Holy Roman Emperor. Invading armies from the north had to skirt the almost impassable Apennines, rising to the west, and often came down this side where they faced stout resistance from Papal troops and mercenaries.

For long a wild region, underpopulated except for the coast, there are few ancient towns to correspond to the hilltowns of Umbria. Settlement really began in the 15th century, once powerful warlords had established territories – miniature kingdoms – on behalf of the Pope or Emperor, providing a degree of stability.

Camerino and Fabriano

Camerino was one of the earliest feudal territories to be established, the stronghold of the Varano family from around 1260 to 1539. The **Varano castle** survives as a picturesque ruin high above the town and the stability provided by the family enabled a proto-university, the Studio Camerinese, to be established as early as the 14th century. The University was officially recognised in 1727 and today the town's best buildings belong to the various faculties.

The town's churches are either monstrous and missable or under restoration, but the best works of art have been gathered together in the **Diocesan Museum** (open Tues and Sat 10.00–13.00) in the Palazzo Arcivescovile. The exhibits here include 13th-century wooden statues from rural churches in the region, embroidered vestments and Tiepolo's *Madonna appearing to St Philip Neri*.

The **Palazzo Ducale** is now the main university building and the restored 15th-century cloister leads to a terrace with outstanding views over the Botanical Garden, first planted in 1828 (open daily except Sat and public holidays, 9.00–12.00, 15.00–18.00).

The 13th-century church of **San Francesco** now serves as the town museum and art gallery (open July–Sept, 9.00–13.00, 17.00–20.00). Quite apart from the delicate vaulting of the apse the church contains a number of accomplished frescoes by the local artist Girolamo di Giovanni, who painted his *Annunciation* and *Madonna and Child* in the late 15th century.

From Camerino there is a choice of routes to San Severino Marche. Perhaps the most scenic road is the N77, which follows the River Chienti and the shores of Lake Pievefavera, followed by the mountain road that climbs to Serrapetrona.

San Severino

San Severino is really two towns. The medieval quarter, known as Il Castello, stands high above the River Potenza on the peak of Montenero, commanding magnificent views up and down the valley. Here the **Duomo Vecchio**, the old cathedral, is a patchwork of 11th-, 14th- and 17th-century masonry, with a 15th-century cloister added for good measure and fragments of early 15th-century frescoes by Lorenzo Salimbeni.

Most of San Severino's inhabitants now live in the new town down in the valley, established in the late 14th century. One of the oldest buildings is the 15th-century **Palazzo Tacchi-Venturi**, which now houses the Museo Archeologico and Pinacoteca (open 9.00–13.30 and, in July–Sept, 16.30–18.30, closed Mon).

Roman finds from the city of Septempeda, San Severino's predecessor, are displayed on the ground floor while the excellent art gallery on the first floor displays works by Pinturicchio, Crivelli and the brothers Lorenzo and Iacomo Salimbeni. These last two artists, born in San Severino, led the revival of painting in the Marches in the late 14th century, principally through their work for the Dukes of Urbino. One of the best and most colourful examples of Lorenzo's work is the *Marriage of St Catherine* triptych displayed here in Room 3. The last room contains fine intarsia-work choir stalls that were once in the Duomo Vecchio, made between 1483 and 1513.

The **new cathedral**, with its Gothic brick portal dating to 1473, is one of the buildings grouped around the main square, the Piazza del Popolo, along with several 16th-century palazzi.

The River Potenza, which flows through the broad valley of San Severino, has long been used as a source of pure water for papermaking. West of San Severino, at Pioraco, the river has been canalised to supply both the modern and more ancient paper mills that are perched on narrow terraces above an attractive gorge.

Fabriano

Twenty-seven kilometres to the north of San Severino lies Fabriano, the main centre of the paper industry. To reach it you pass through the light industrial town of **Matelica** – not an attractive place but worth a brief stop for the buildings around the central square, the Piazza Enrico Mattei. The buildings include the 13th-century Palazzo Pretorio and the 15th-century Palazzo Ottoni, home of the family that once ruled the town. The scene is somewhat marred by the dominant Neo-Baroque façade of the Chiesa del Suffragio. The Museo Piersanti (Via Umberto I 11, open 10.00–12.00, 17.00–19.00 in summer, 16.00–18.00 in winter, closed Mon) is full of Flemish tapestries, carpets, silverware, furniture and paintings dating from the 15th to the 19th centuries.

Fabriano has few buildings of beauty; the best is the gaunt Palazzo del Podestà (1255) in the Piazza del Comune, fronted by the elegant fountain of 1285, a simplified version of Perugia's Fontana Maggiore without the sculpture. The Duomo, largely rebuilt in 1617, is interesting for one of Salvator Rosa's earliest works, *St Nicholas of Tolentino*.

The main reason for coming to Fabriano is the interesting Museo della Carta e della Filigrana (Museum of Paper and Watermarks) housed in the restored convent of San Domenico in Via Baldo, south of the Duomo (open 9.00–12.00, 15.00–18.00 Tues–Sat, 15.00–18.00 Sun, closed Mon).

Papermills are recorded in Fabriano as early as the 13th century and the town claims to have invented the watermark. Today's mills specialise in the high-quality papers used for making banknotes – those of Italy and of her former colonies. The museum charts the history of papermaking in the region and demonstrations of the basic processes are given regularly, using equipment dating from an age when papermaking was still a handicraft.

Nearly 18km north-east of Fabriano, down the busy N76, a turning to the left leads to the spectacular limestone gorge cut by the River Sentina and called the **Gola di Frasassi**. A large and unmissable car park serves the Grotte di

Frasassi, the most extensive system of caves in Italy. The caves were discovered only in 1971 and are still being explored. It is known that they extend for at least 13km under Mount Frasassi and may link up with other cave systems stretching for a total of 35km.

Guided tours take place every hour, on the hour, and follow a circular walk of 1.6km. Tour leaders will point out numerous spotlit stalactites and stalagmites given names suggested by their shapes but even this folksy approach does not detract from the awesome splendour of this subterranean world or the sheer size of the main cave, the Grotta Grande del Vento, the Great Cave of the Wind.

Not far from the cave car park is the beautiful 11th-century church of **San Vittore delle Chiuse**, one of the oldest and best-preserved churches in the Marches. Apart from the gaunt 13th-century campanile the rest of the church is a delicate structure with a lovely octagonal central tower, covered in blank arcading. The side apses ringing the nave and sanctuary are an unusual feature associated with Byzantine-inspired architecture.

The little hamlet of **Genga**, nearby, is worth a stop for the late 15th-century triptych by Antonio da Fabriano in the church of San Clemente, before heading on to Sassoferrato.

Sassoferrato and the central Marches

Sassoferrato

The name of this attractive town may be familiar as the birthplace of G. B. Salvi, better known as Sassoferrato, who was one of the most prolific Italian painters of the 17th century. The town was also the site of a decisive battle, in 295BC, when the Roman army defeated the combined forces of the Samnites and the Gauls. The ruins of the Roman town of Sentinum, where the battle took place, can be visited in the southern outskirts.

Like so many Marches towns, Sassoferrato consists of both a modern and an ancient settlement. The medieval town, built on a wooded hilltop 2km east of the modern town, features the 12th-century church of Santa Croce, built of masonry salvaged from Roman Sentinum, as well as a public park created around the walls of the 14th-century fortress.

The lower town is made interesting by a number of museums. The best is the **Museo Civico**, housed in the 16th-century Palazzo dei Priori (open March –June 9.30–12.30, 15.00–18.00; July–Sept 9.30–12.30, 16.00–19.00) where you can see further archaeological finds from Sentinum, but you can also visit two museums devoted, respectively, to the traditional and the contemporary arts of the Marches, in the Palazzo Montanari (Via Montanari, same hours as the Museo Civico).

The towns of the central and coastal regions

From Sassoferrato you can also explore the central and coastal regions of the Marches, if you are determined to tour comprehensively. **Jesi**, to the east, is an industrial city in which you are bound to get lost searching for the Renaissance Palazzo della Signoria (Piazza Angelo Colocci), which houses the Museo Archaeologico, or the Pinacoteca in the Palazzo Pianetti (be warned, both are under rearrangement and sections may be closed).

Cingoli, south of Jesi, is famed for its views east to the Adriatic and is therefore known as the 'balcone delle Marche', the balcony of the Marches.

Ancona is a bustling port and modern city, rebuilt after heavy bombing in World War II and an earthquake in 1972, but has one outstanding monument: the 11th-century Romanesque cathedral, built on a hilltop at the tip of the harbour on the site of a Roman temple to Venus.

At **Loreto** everything you would want to see is grouped around the broad Piazza della Madonna. The Gothic cathedral, begun in the 15th century but not completed until the 18th, shelters the house in which the Virgin was born and in which Jesus lived until the age of 30. One story explaining its presence here says that angels transported it from the Holy Land; another credits crusaders with dismantling the house and shipping it from Nazareth to Loreto in the late 13th century. In any event, it is a major pilgrimage centre, second in popularity only to the Vatican City, and the cathedral is embellished with numerous works of art dating from the 16th century onwards.

Recanati is devoted to a tourist industry based on the fact that Italy's best known modern poet, Giacomo Leopardi, was born there; the city's other famous son, the operatic tenor Benjamino Gigli, comes out second best and is acknowledged only by a display of memorabilia in the Pinacoteca.

Opera is the principal attraction of **Macerata**. The impressive Arena Sferisterio, able to accommodate an audience of 7,500, was built in the 1820s and is the setting for an opera festival held every July when leading singers entertain the crowds with popular arias.

Finally, **Tolentino** is rescued from ugliness by the magnificent Basilica di San Nicola, dedicated to St Nicholas who was born in the town in 1245; his story is told in remarkable frescoes dating to 1330 and there is a beautifully planted 14th-century cloister alongside. In September, in odd-numbered years, the town is host to an international festival of humorous art.

Practical Information

Tourist information offices

ANCONA
Corso Stamira 60.

CAMERINO
Vico del Comune 1.

CINGOLE
Via L. Ferri 4.

FABRIANO
Piazza del Comune 42.

JESI
Piazza della Repubblica 9.

LORETO
Via Solari 3.

MACERATA
Piazza Libertà 12.

MATELICA
Piazza E. Mattei 3.

NORCIA
Piazza San Bendetto.

SAN SEVERINO MARCHE
Piazza del Popolo.

SASSOFERRATO
Via C. Battista 13.

TOLENTINO
Piazza Libertà 17.

Where to stay

ARCEVIA
Alle Terrazze, Via Rocchi (tel. 0731-9395). Just 12km north east of Sassoferrato, this is one of the best hotels in the Marches, in a fine woodland setting just outside Arcevia with a pool and tennis court and the town's best restaurant.

CASTELLUCCIO
Sibilla (tel. 0743-870113). The only place you can stay in this tiny hamlet, a simple *pensione* with a restaurant specialising in dishes made from the sweet locally-grown lentils.

FABRIANO
Janus Hotel, Piazza Matteotti 45 (tel. 0732-4191). A first-class hotel with a good restaurant but closed in August.
Aristos, Via Cavour 103 (tel. 0732-22308). The inexpensive alternative, but with no restaurant.

JESI
Federico II, Via Ancona (tel. 0731-343 641). A luxury hotel, with international standard facilities and prices to match, on the outskirts of the town.

NORCIA
Grotta Azzura, Via Alfieri 12 (tel. 0743 816513), or **Posta**, Via C. Battista 10 (tel. 0743 816 724). Both hotels face each other just off Norcia's central square and, with little to choose between them in terms of price and comfort, the Grotta Azzura wins marginally for its restaurant.

Where to eat

FABRIANO
Pollo, Via Corridoni 22 (tel. 0732-24584). The best restaurant locally for regional specialities (closed Tues).

NORCIA
Galeazzi, Via Mura Occidentale 5 (tel. 0731-57944). Highly regarded and specialising in regional dishes and local Verdicchio wines (closed Mon and August).
Also **Grotta Azzura** and **Posta**, see above.

12. GUBBIO AND THE NORTH

From Sassoferrato to Gualdo Tadino

Heading westwards out of Sassoferrato, the N360 climbs up the Sentino valley to **Isola Fossara**. In this village a winding by-road on the right leads through beautiful wooded countryside until, after about 3km, you reach the semi-ruinous **Abbazia di Santa Maria di Sitria**, with its restored 11th-century church sitting on top of a 6th-century crypt.

Continue on for another 10km and you will reach an even more remote abbey, the **Eremo di Fonte Avellana**. This hermitage, surrounded by oak woods and mountain pasture, was founded in AD980. Off the graceful Romanesque cloister you can visit the original monastic cells, one of which gave shelter to Dante around 1310 when he was wandering in exile from his native Florence and conceiving various forms of poetic torture to which he condemned his enemies in Hell. The hermitage was an important medieval centre of learning and the Dante Alighieri library, named in honour of the poet's visit, occupies the former scriptorium where manuscripts were laboriously copied by hand.

Back in the Sentino valley, the N360 heads west to meet the N3, the Via Flaminia, at Scheggia on the Umbrian side of the border. Turn and follow the N3 through a fertile plain with the flat-topped mountains rising like a cliff to the left. The mountains can be explored by taking the left turn in Sigillo. After 9km this scenic road comes out near the summit of Umbria's highest peak, **Monte Cucco** (1,566m). The mountain meadows here make a popular picnic spot for local people in the summer.

A short walk back down the same track, at Ranco di Sigillo, is an entrance to an extraordinary cave system that penetrates deep into the mountain, reaching to a depth of almost 1km. On occasions during the summer one of the more accessible caves, the Grotta di Monte Cucco, is open to the public.

Gualdo Tadino

Further south is the bustling town of Gualdo Tadino. The Roman city of Tadinum, a staging post along the Via Flaminia, lay in the plain and was virtually destroyed by Totila the Goth as his forces swept down through Italy towards Rome. Totila also met his end here, killed in AD442 by the Byzantine commander Narses beneath the ruined walls of the city.

A new city – Gualdo Tadino, meaning 'wooded Tadino', from the Lombardic *wald*, or wood – was built higher up to enjoy the relative safety of the hilltops. It is a stiff climb from the car park outside the city walls up to the **Rocca Flea**, the 13th-century fortress built under the rule of the Holy Roman Emperor Frederick II and now a cultural centre. South of the Rocca is Gualdo Tadino's unpretentious main square, the Piazza dei Martiri della Libertà, with its memorial to partisans who, operating in the surrounding hills, put up brave resistance to the Nazis in World War II. Here are the town's most imposing buildings. The **Duomo**, closing the eastern side of the square, has a fine rose window and Romanesque portal dating to 1256. Sadly, the interior, remodelled in 1752 and again in the 19th century, is characterless and contains only illuminated wax effigies of local saints.

All the works of art from the Duomo are now displayed in the nearby church of **San Francesco**, converted to form the Pinacoteca Comunale. Still under restoration, this church is likely to be closed but the key may be obtained from the police station (Vigili Urbani) in the same square. Gathered in the church are several works by the local artist, Matteo da Gualdo, including his delightful *Madonna and Child*, and a polyptych by Nicolo Alunno, painted in 1471 and considered his masterpiece.

Several shops in this small town are devoted to the *caccia*, hunting, and sell the guns and accessories that no self-respecting Italian huntsman would be seen without. The hills around Gualdo Tadino are safe enough, however, since hunting is strictly controlled, and you will not be in danger of a stray shot if you take the lovely road up to **Valsorda**, where the mountain pastures are bright with the sky-blue of chicory, the yellow of broom, the pink of perennial sweet-peas and campion and the white of ox-eye daisies. An easy-to-follow track leads to the summit of the Serra Santa (1421m) with its little pilgrim church and outstanding views.

Other shops in Gualdo Tadino sell reproductions of ancient Etruscan ceramics, but the main centre of this industry is at Gubbio, 24km to the north west along the N219.

Gubbio

The opportunity to buy locally made black burnished *bucchera* vases, modelled on graceful Etruscan prototypes, is not the least of the several attractions of this fascinating town.

Gubbio was dubbed the 'city of silence' by the poet d'Annunzio because

Gubbio, the City of Silence, rises in a series of terraces above the remains of its Roman amphitheatre in the plain below

it was, for many centuries, isolated and in decline. Not so any more, for the wide plain below the walls is now full of light industrial factories; these form a disappointing prelude to old Gubbio, but the atmosphere within the city walls is entirely different. The tall austere buildings seem as ancient as time. They have been pounded and rebuilt so many times that they are all now a patchwork of masonry of different dates with blocked windows and doorways, later ones cutting through earlier ones, forming an archaeologist's paradise. Battered wooden doors open to reveal modern, comfortable interiors. It was such a feat of engineering to put these buildings up in the first place, perched on narrow terraces up the steep face of Mount Ingino, that nobody would be foolish enough to demolish them and start again. Instead, each time the city was attacked and left semi-ruinous, new buildings were constructed by patching up the old.

The Romans were the last to do any substantial remodelling, building their town of Iguvium above the site of the ancient Umbrian town of Tota Ikuvina. The Roman legacy consists of the rectilinear street pattern, the walls and town

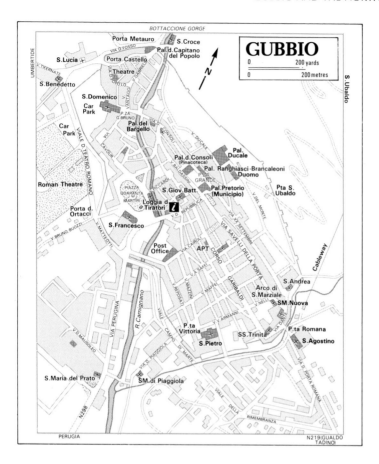

gates and the well-preserved 1st-century AD **amphitheatre** in the plain just
south of the city (off the Viale dei Teatro Romano), still used for summer
theatrical performances.

When the town was partly destroyed by Totila the Goth, the Gubbians
responded in the same way as other Umbrian victims of the barbarian invaders
and shifted the focus of the town higher up the hill. To do so involved con-
structing the two narrow terraces on which the principal buildings sit, shored
up by cliff-like walls over 20m high.

The scale of this achievement can best be appreciated from the **Giardini
Pensili**, a small garden in front of the Palazzo Ducale, which offers vertiginous
views down over the cascading rooftops of the medieval town. The **Palazzo
Ducale** itself has just been restored and you can enter the delightful inner
courtyard, with its graceful Renaissance arcades, an unexpected architectural
treat hidden behind the austere façade.

157

The Palazzo was a relatively late addition to the town, commissioned in 1476 by Federico di Montefeltro, Duke of Urbino, after he had been invited to protect the town and its citizens following their rebellion against papal rule. The palazzo was built on the sight of a much older Lombard palace in which, according to local tradition, the Emperor Charlemagne stayed in the early 9th century, following his coronation in Rome by Pope Leo III.

Likewise the **Duomo**, alongside the Palazzo, stands on much older foundations, rebuilt in the 13th century. The simple façade has lost its rose window but retains the surrounding sculptures of the Lamb of God and the Evangelists. The serene interior resembles one of the great communal tents of the Marsh Arabs of central Iraq, with ten great skeletal stone arches rising from the nave piers like the rib-bones of a whale.

The Gothic east window glows with the colours of much-restored 13th-century stained glass, depicting saints in niches, and the transepts are filled with magnificently carved and painted 16th-century cantoria, or choir lofts. An ancient Roman sarcophagus is just visible in the dim light below the main altar. The greatest treasure of the church was a 16th-century Flemish cope embroidered with scenes from the Passion and given to Gubbio by Pope Marcellus, a native of the town; sadly, part of the cope was stolen in 1990 and the Museum has been closed ever since.

Descending from the cathedral, the human scale of Gubbio is apparent in the long, steep stone staircases that link the narrow main streets. Even the red-paved principal square, the Piazza della Signoria, is small by comparison with that of many towns of similar size. One side of the square is open to the sky and offers breathtaking views. The western side is filled by the noble 14th-century **Palazzo dei Consoli**, one of the more ornate town halls in Umbria. The Gubbian architect, Gattapone, the builder of Spoleto's fortress and Ponte della Torri, is credited with the construction of this palace; a suggestion that seems to be contradicted by the inscription over the main entrance stating the Angelo da Orvieto was the architect. Perhaps Gattapone was responsible for the massive superstructure and Angelo for the prettier details – the doorways and the fan staircase that leads up to the main hall.

The upper part, with its pairs of windows linked by a dentil frieze, the blank arcading below the battlements and the finger-like campanile all belong to a later phase of building. The lower storey, with its pilaster strips, dates from 1321–1350, the upper storey to the early 16th century, though still distinctly medieval in style. High on the buttress on the right of the façade is an iron cage in which criminals were once exposed to the ferocity of the sun and the ridicule of all Gubbio.

If you have already visited the Palazzo dei Priori in Perugia or, further afield, the town halls of Florence and Siena, the interior of Gubbio's palazzo will come as a surprise; instead of gorgeously frescoed walls and ceilings you enter a vast barrel-vaulted hall with bare stone walls, in fact the original untouched 14th-century council chamber. Functional as it is, the chamber did not lack amenities. Gubbio was one of the first cities in Umbria to organise a domestic water supply, piped to individual palazzi; the jumble of masonry ranged around the walls of this chamber include several examples of early stone toilet seats and basins.

The **Pinacoteca** is housed upstairs, in the early 16th-century rooms above the chamber, many of which have not been touched since they were built. There are very few great works of art here – the best work, Fiorentino's *Madonna of the Pomegranate*, was stolen in 1979 and has not been recovered. The most significant items in the collection are easily overlooked. The Eugubine Tablets consist of seven dull bronze sheets (an eighth has been lost) inscribed with what is, to our eyes, unintelligible script. The tablets were found in 1444 in a field close to Gubbio's Roman amphitheatre and the text, written in a mixture of Etruscan and Latin characters, describes religious rites, forms of prayer and liturgical regulations practised by a local college of priests, the Atiedii. The earliest of the tablets dates from the 3rd century BC and the later ones from the 1st century BC but they were found together and perhaps represent an attempt by the Romans to record and understand the religious practices of the local people – or, as some scholars have argued, vice versa: to introduce their own concepts of augury and divination to this part of Umbria.

If nothing else in the picture gallery captures your attention, do not miss the door in the main hall that leads out on to a small loggia added to the south side of the palazzo in the 16th century. From here there are dizzying views over the rooftops of Gubbio.

From the palace, turn left and left again, down Via dei Consoli, to reach the **Palazzo del Bargello**, a 13th-century former prison with several characteristic medieval features. The windows and doors have typically Umbrian depressed arches and, to the left of the façade, there is a *porta del morto*, with its step several feet above pavement level. Several nearby houses have similar doors, some of them now blocked, and tradition has it that these 'doors of the dead' were used exclusively for the passage of coffins; it was considered inauspicious to take a coffin through the main entrance, so these little doorways were made and only unblocked in the event of a death occurring in the household.

That, at least, is the story. The truth, as always, is more prosaic. The main door, at street level, leads into the storage area of the house. The higher door led to the living quarters. At night, and in times of trouble, the wooden steps leading to the higher door could be withdrawn and the narrow door itself barred securely. Would-be intruders, mistaking the street level door for the main entrance, would find themselves in the courtyard or cellars and liable to bombardment from above.

The **Fontana dei Matti** (Fountain of the Mad) stands in front of the Bargello and is so named because it was once believed that you would go mad if you waded round the basin three times. It is open to question whether anyone who did this might not already be mad. Today, on high days and holidays, young men wade around the fountain to qualify as 'honorary madmen of Gubbio'.

South of the Bargello, the River Camignano flows down the side of the street of the same name, and if you follow the river you will emerge in the

The Bargello, or Prison, and the Fontana dei Matti (Fountain of the Mad) in Gubbio

wide, oval-shaped **Piazza Quaranta Martiri** (the Square of the Forty Martyrs, commemorating 40 Gubbian women and children shot on 22 June 1944 in retaliation for an attack on the retreating Nazis by members of the Italian Resistance). Happier scenes fill the square today; the Logge di Tiratori, the Weavers' Loggia, on the north side of the square, is now a fruit and vegetable market. The loggia was built in the 14th century for protecting cloth, after washing and fulling, from the heat of the sunshine as it was laid out on racks to dry.

On the opposite side of the square the church of **San Francesco** also offers a welcome retreat from the sun. The simple church, with its slender Gothic piers, has been restored to its 13th-century appearance. The apse of the north aisle (left-hand side) contains outstanding early Renaissance frescoes on the life of the Virgin, painted by Ottaviano Nelli in 1408–13. Restoration has revealed the gorgeous colours and rich detail of these lively scenes.

Off the south aisle, opposite, the presbytery incorporates the walls of a 13th-century house belonging to Jacobo Spada, with whom St Francis stayed when he visited Gubbio and tamed a wolf that had been terrorising the town; it is said that St Francis charmed the wolf into behaving in a more gentle manner in return for regular meals provided by the people of Gubbio.

The quiet shady cloister nearby is used to display some 1st-century AD Roman mosaics of Neptune, Cupid and seahorses, and the cloister shop sells very fine reproductions of Renaissance majolica made by local craftsmen. The ceramics industry in Gubbio began in the Middle Ages and reached its brief zenith in the 16th century when Giorgio Andreoli da Intra discovered the secret of making a ruby-red glaze – a formula he refused to pass on so that the secret died with him and was only rediscovered this century.

If the frescoes in San Francesco give you an appetite for more of Ottaviano Nelli's work, you should seek out two more churches in the western part of the city, near the Porta Romana. Santa Maria Nuova, in Via Nelli, contains his best work, the *Madonna of the Belvedere* (1403), while Sant' Agostino, just outside the same gate, has his *Last Judgement* (1420).

Alongside Sant' Agostino a cable car station will save you the long haul up Mount Ingino to the **Basilica of Sant' Ubaldo** on the summit (827m). The basilica, nothing special in itself, houses the relics of the patron saint of Gubbio, Bishop Ubaldo, whose miraculous intervention defended the city from attack in the 12th century. Here too are the extraordinary *ceri*, or candles, that are carried in the race held to commemorate his feast day. Looking at these great timber structures you realise what courage and stamina is required by the teams who race from the cathedral in the town below up to this basilica with the candles on their shoulders.

From Gubbio to Urbino

The most straightforward route to Urbino is the scenic N452 which joins the N3, the Via Flaminia, at Pontericcioli. The N3 then heads north along the Burano valley. Just north of Pontedazzo, you can divert north along the old road that runs parallel to the modern highway to see the complete double-arched Roman bridge that still carries local traffic two millennia after it was built. **Cagli** merits a brief stop for the Romanesque church of San Francesco, its 13th-century Palazzo Comunale and its well-preserved Rocca, built in 1481 in the old part of the town.

For a more spectacular route, head westwards out of Gubbio on the N219 and then north, after 8km, turning right up the mountain road that leads to Pietralunga. The road passes through some of Umbria's wildest and most scenic countryside, one moment twisting through wooded hills, the next passing over high, bare mountain pastures grazed by sheep and goats. If you follow the signs from Pietralunga to Apecchio, you will cross the plains that surround Pian di Serra and descend to join the N257.

Heading east from Apecchio, with the heights of Mount Nerone (1525m) to your right, you pass through the gorge cut by the Torrente Biscubio. Piobbico is an attractive medieval village dominated by the 13th-century Castello Brancaleoni.

Both routes join at **Acqualagna**. This town is the centre of the local white truffle trade but not worth a stop unless you happen to be passing in the autumn early enough in the morning to catch the markets where the precious *funghi* are displayed for sale.

North of Acqualagna you should take the narrow road that runs parallel with the N3 and the River Candigliano. Just outside the town, the **Abbazia San Vincenzo al Furlo** stands on the right-hand side of the road, a simple Lombardic church built in 1042 and floored with great slabs of the abundant local limestone. Patches of delicate 13th-century fresco remain on the walls and the only other adornment is an 11th-century angel carved on the left-hand entrance to the crypt.

Just beyond the abbey church you pass through **Furlo**, a village of stone-masons' yards where great raw slabs of limestone wait to be sawn into paving stones and building blocks. Then you enter the dramatic Furlo gorge (Gola di Furlo), so narrow that there is just room for the road and the river between the great cliffs of limestone. The green-blue waters of the River Candigliano no longer swirl with the furious torrent that cut this gorge, undermining the cliffs and hollowing out caves at their base. Instead it has been damned and flows so calmly and silently that any noise echoes up the bare rock faces.

At the northern end, the narrowest point of the gorge, the road passes through a short tunnel, cut through the rock in 76–77AD. An inscription on the northern entrance to the tunnel records its excavation during the reign of the Emperor Vespasian and, if you can find a safe place to park along the narrow road, you can examine the tunnel sides for the Roman chisel marks in the rock, and climb to the little church perched above the tunnel entrance. The tunnel gave its name to the gorge: *furlo* is a corruption of the Latin *forulus*, a hole in the rock.

After this quiet and atmospheric spot you either pass beneath the N3 and head straight for Urbino or take the busy Via Flaminia and detour to **Fossombrone**, principally for the Museo Civico; housed in the 15th-century Corte Alta, the mansion of the Malatestas, this contains archaeological finds from Fossombrone's Roman predecessor, Forum Sempronii.

Practical Information

Tourist information offices

GUALDO TADINO
Via Calai 39.

GUBBIO
Piazza Odersi 6 (tel. 075 9220693).

Where to stay

GUBBIO
Bosone, Via 20 Septembre 22 (tel. 075-927 2008). In the upper town by the cathedral, with fine views and a hotel garage (closed Feb).
Gattapone, Via Beni 11 (tel. 075-927 2489). Pleasant, central and inexpensive, with a small garden (closed 7 Jan–6 Feb).
San Marco, Via Perugina 5 (tel. 074-927 2349). Large, modern and comfortable, but just outside the city walls.

Where to eat

GUALDO TADINO
Ristorante Gigiotto, Via Morone 5 (tel. 075-912 283). A huge, family-run restaurant specialising in roast lamb and local cheeses (closed Weds, except July and Aug, and 5–20 Nov).

GUBBIO
Taverna del Lupo, Via Ansidei 21A (tel. 075-927 1269). Named after the wolf tamed by St Francis, this large but atmospheric restaurant in a medieval setting specialises in local game and truffle-flavoured pastas (closed Mon and 7 Jan –6 Feb).
Fornace di Mastro Giorgio, Via della Fornace di Mastro Giorgio (tel. 075-927 5740). This restaurant occupies the former workshop in which, by tradition, Gubbio's most famous potter created his ruby-red glazes. This theme is slightly overdone in the décor but the excellent food ranges from local specialities, such as pigeon with olives, to fresh fish and seafood (available on Thurs and Fri only. Restaurant closed Mon and 4–28 Feb).
Porta Tessenaca, Via Picardi 21 (tel. 075-927 2765). Close to the Palazzo Consoli in the heart of the city and set in a 15th-century hall; popular with visitors and sometimes hectic.
Pizzeria Il Bargello, Via dei Consoli 37. Best choice for cheaper eats, with polenta and lamb dishes available as well as traditional pizza.

13. URBINO

Urbino, the highlight of the Marches region, is a unique and fascinating city; unique because nowhere else in Italy is the palace of its ruling family so completely integrated with the city itself. Urbino has long been described as a palace-city for this very reason; there seems to be no precise point at which the Ducal Palace stops and the city begins. The walls of the palace extend to embrace the city and the mellow rose-coloured brick from which most of Urbino is built adds further to the sense of homogeneity.

It is a city, too, that seems to have one foot in this century and another in the historic past. The people that gather in the traffic-free main square of an evening, to talk and watch Urbino's gentle sunsets, are urbane and cultured. Many are teachers or students at the city's ancient university, founded in 1508. They are the direct heirs, in a sense, of the poets, painters, artists and humanists who gathered at the court of the Montefeltro family in the 15th century.

There is a real sense of continuity between that time and this. Even though the Montefeltro line died out in 1508 and despite the fact that many of Urbino's artistic treasures are now scattered far and wide – notably in Florence, Rome, London, Paris and St Petersburg – the city retains the appearance that the Duke of Urbino, Federico di Montefeltro, gave it during his long reign (1444–1482). In this respect it is sobering to reflect that Urbino was nearly blasted to destruction in August 1944 when retreating Nazis mined the walls; fortunately very few of the mines exploded and British bomb disposal teams worked heroically, after the Liberation, to defuse the remainder.

Urbino looks a complex city at first sight, though finding your orientation is quite simple. The principal landmark, indeed the glory of the city, is the west wing of the Ducal Palace, with its famous 'Facciata dei Torricini' – the façade of the towers. This façade rises five storeys high out of the steep hillside. Slender cylindrical towers, topped by spires, lend the city, viewed from this side, the appearance of a romantic fairy-tale castle. Between the towers a series of loggias, framed by triumphal arches and carved out of white limestone, contrasts with the red brick and climbs the full height of the façade.

The main car park, in the Piazzale Mercatale, lies just below this entrancing façade and the nearby gate, the Porta di Valbona, leads straight into the main street, the Via Mazzini. At the top of this wide road is the main square, the Piazza della Repubblica. This scarcely level plain sits between two hills. The Via Raffaello, to the left, leads to the summit of one; the Via V. Veneto, to

The approach to Urbino is dominated by the bulk of the cathedral and the Palazzo Ducale with its twin towers

the right, leads to the cathedral, Ducal Palace and University at the peak of the other. Together these two hills gave Urbino its name: Urbs Bina, meaning 'double town'. Around these principal arteries tiny cobbled alleys lead off in every direction, but never far before meeting the 16th-century walls, for Urbino is a very compact city.

The Palazzo Ducale

Taking the right-hand road, the Via V. Veneto, you quickly reach the main goal of most visitors to Urbino, the Palazzo Ducale. Viewed from the square beside the cathedral, the palace presents an untidy exterior; raw brickwork, with putlock holes for supporting the original scaffolding still visible, rises above an unfinished stretch of rusticated limestone walling.

As with many Renaissance buildings, the façade was left to be finished last; often, given the timescales involved and the massive costs, the façade was never completed, either because the original patron had died or because the money had run out. The unfinished state of this building nevertheless enables us to read something of its constructional history. The long wing that runs up

165

one side of Piazza Rinascimento is pierced by a series of Gothic round-headed windows. This wing represents the old Palazzo delle Jole, which already stood on the site when Duke Federico commissioned his new palace.

The first architect, Maso di Bartolomeo, began work in 1450 by extending and modifying the existing buildings. The next architect to have a hand in the project was Luciano Laurana, who is credited with the majority of the new building and worked here from 1465 to 1474.

Francesco di Giorgio Martini then took over and brought the palace near to completion, commissioning Ambrogio Barocci to design the handsome classical windows and portals that we see on the façade facing the cathedral. Work then stopped abruptly with Duke Federico's death in 1482. The upper storey of the palace was not completed until the first half of the 16th century, under the architect Girolamo Genga, and slight differences can be detected in the brickwork below the eaves, representing this final stage of building.

The public entrance to the palace (usually open 9.00–12.00, closed Mon) is through a door in the right-hand façade, facing the cathedral. It is an insignificant entrance but leads into a remarkably elegant courtyard, consisting of a four-sided portico with slender Corinthian columns supporting hemispherical arches. The work of Luciano Laurana, this noble courtyard dates to 1480 and has been hailed as one of the most perfect examples of Renaissance classical architecture in all of Italy – much copied by subsequent palace builders.

A Latin inscription, in handsome lettering, runs around the two upper friezes and records the many titles that Duke Federico inherited or acquired by means of his military exploits; it goes on to record that, after defeating many enemies in battle, he settled to the life of a humanist, patron and scholar, and that 'justice, clemency, liberality and religion tempered and embellished his victories in times of peace.'

Federico was, in fact, the penultimate member of the Montefeltro family to rule the city. Urbino, settled by the Lombards, was one of the five cities in the Marches that Charlemagne conceded to Pope Leo III in AD800 as part of the price he paid for being acknowledged officially as Holy Roman Emperor. These same cities rebelled against papal rule in the early 12th century and declared themselves independent, self-governing communities. In the Guelph –Ghibelline conflicts, Urbino was on the side of the pro-imperial Ghibellines and it was the Emperor Frederick Barbarossa who appointed the Montefeltri to govern Urbino on his behalf.

Duke Federico succeeded in 1444, and early in his career won the support of the Pope by fighting in his support. Later, as the inscription boasts, he retired to Urbino as a renowned and humane ruler, head of a court which Castiglione, in *The Courtier*, idealised as the most civilised in Europe.

A famous portrait (now in the Uffizi in Florence), painted by Piero della Francesca around 1460 to celebrate the Duke's marriage to Battista Sforza, shows a heavy-jowled, hook-nosed man (his nose was broken in battle). The main staircase of the palace has another likeness; this time a statue carved by

Campagna in the 17th century, which idealises the Duke and portrays him as an august figure in Roman military armour.

The doorway at the top of the staircase, the Porta della Guerra, is a magnificent work. The design of the intarsia-work doorways and marble doorcase, delicately carved with military emblems, was the work of the wandering Sienese artist, Francesco di Giorgio Martini and executed around 1475.

This door leads into the living quarters of the palace, now serving as the **National Gallery of the Marches** and displaying what remains in Urbino of the works of art that the Montefeltri owned or commissioned. There are few highlights to look out for in this frequently reorganised collection.

Piero della Francesca's *Flagellation*, stolen in 1976 but now returned, is a strange painting by a man whose obsession with the mathematics of linear perspective drove him to the brink of insanity. The complex symbolism of this picture, mixing pagan and Christian elements, continues to be the subject of academic debate. The three figures in the foreground, ignoring the scourging of Christ behind them, have been interpreted as representing relatives of the Duke discussing the fate of the decadent Church. The same artist's *Senigallia Madonna* is an equally mystical work, noted for its use of subtle and muted colours.

The Ideal City, painted by Luciano Laurana, the architect of the palace, is another renowned example of the application of linear perspective, this time to depict three sides of a piazza with a circular temple-like structure at its centre. The painting shows the type of classically inspired buildings that Renaissance architects aspired to build, though they rarely had the opportunity to do so on such a grand scale. It is also a rare example of a studio piece, perhaps painted more in the spirit of experiment rather than with the intention of public display.

Another great treasure to look out for is the delightful *Portrait of a Gentlewoman* known as 'La Muta', painted by Raphael and perhaps representing Maddelena Doni. This gentle and beautiful picture is one of the handful painted by Raphael that remain in his native city.

Perhaps more rewarding than the works of art are the furnishings of the palace, especially in those rooms that Duke Federico reserved for his own use. These lie to the rear of the building, in the angle between the two western turrets. The best and most famous of these is Duke Federico's study, called by the diminutive, '**Studiolo**', because of its small size. The irregularly shaped room measures approximately 3.6m square, but it seems much larger because of the high ceiling and the *trompe l'oeil* panelling that gives the illusion of depth.

Although the smallest room in the palace, it is also the richest. The magnificent coffered ceiling is covered in heraldic devices and an inscription giving the various titles of Duke Federico: Duke of Urbino, Count of Montefeltro and Casteldurante, Gonfalonier of the Holy Roman Church, and so on.

Below, ranked in two tiers, are 28 portraits of the scholars, philosophers, poets, lawgivers, orators and intellectuals that Duke Federico most admired – most of them with book in hand; the missing ones, replaced by copies in monochrome, are now in the Louvre in Paris. We can imagine that, if the Duke's mind ever wandered from his studies, he would gaze up at his heroes and return to studying his precious Greek and Latin manuscripts with new diligence.

Yet one wonders how the Duke could study at all, surrounded by the distractions of the magnificent intarsia work below. This beautiful wood panelling gives the impression of a room in use and simulates a series of open cupboards. One reveals the Duke's armour, tossed aside as if he had just returned from the battlefield anxious to get back to his studies. Others show books, scientific and musical instruments and sheet music. The most enchanting of all reveals – as if through a window on to a loggia – a distant view of Urbino and, in a wonderful touch of naturalism, a squirrel stealing fruit from a basket that lies on the window sill.

The brilliance of the fully realised perspective and the fine craftsmanship of the intarsia work makes this room one of the outstanding triumphs of the Renaissance. Who was responsible? Scholars still debate the question, but one panel bears the concealed signature of 'Givani Castellano' – perhaps the craftsman, or one of the craftsmen, involved – while the design has been attributed both to Botticelli and to Francesco di Giorgio Martini, the architect who worked on the palace in the 1570s.

Some rooms below the Studiolo are not always open, but you should seek them out if they are. They are reached by descending the spiral staircase within one of the cylindrical towers of the western façade. They include the Duke's bathroom, or garderobe, the barrel-vaulted **Temple of the Muses** (sadly minus the frescoes that once adorned the walls) and the exquisite **Cappella del Perdono**, the Chapel of Forgiveness, whose walls, lined with precious marbles and stucco ceiling covered with angels' heads, has been attributed to Brabanti. A nearby door leads out on to one of the loggias on the western façade with magnificent views over to the hills surrounding Urbino.

Returning up the stairs, the **Duke's bedroom**, adjoining the Studiolo, usually has a portrait of Federico with his son, Guidobaldo, painted by Pedro Barraguete, the same artist who painted the portraits of illustrious men in the Studiolo itself. This picture is most enjoyable and portrays the Duke relaxing with a book, dressed in armour and wearing the Order of the Garter conferred on him by Edward IV of England, as well as an ermine-trimmed scarlet cloak. He looks every inch the kindly and mildly eccentric father, with his great hooked nose and balding forehead; the son, his face lit radiantly by hope, carries a sceptre as a token that he will one day inherit the Dukedom.

Guidobaldo did succeed in 1482 but was deposed by Cesare Borgia in 1497, only to be restored when the people of Urbino rose against the Borgia army shortly after it invaded the city. An invalid for most of his life, Guidobaldo died without a direct heir and the title passed, in 1508, to his nephew, Francesco delle Rovere.

Francesco proved, like Duke Federico, to be a brave soldier and patron of the arts. He completed the top floor of the palace and this is now used to display works of art and ceramics dating from the 16th century and later. Especially interesting are the ceilings of some of these rooms, decorated with grotesque frescoes, a style that became fashionable after the discovery of this type of Roman ornamentation in the grotto of Nero's garden, excavated in the early 16th century.

Equally fascinating are the rooms in the palace cellars (not always open), especially if you are interested in the domestic economy of a great Renaissance palace. Here you will find the laundry, kitchens, servants' quarters, refrigerators (kept cold by blocks of compressed snow) and elaborate plumbing systems designed to supply central heating and piped hot and cold water to various parts of the palace.

The Palace guest book is also displayed here, usually open at the page signed by 'James III, Re di Gran Bretagna' — James 'the Old Pretender', father of Bonnie Prince Charlie. He fled to Italy after the Battle of Culloden (1745) and eventually settled in Florence under the spurious title 'Count of Albany'.

Several other rooms lead off the central courtyard. The Duke's **Library**, with its ceiling decorated with the Imperial eagle and sunrays, once housed Federico's collection of ancient Greek and Roman manuscripts. These, along with the Duke's finest works of art, were dispersed after the last of the della Rovere line bequeathed the Duchy of Urbino to the Pope in 1626; many of them ended up in the Vatican.

Another room is lined with panels carved by Francesco di Giorgio Martini, illustrating in great detail the tools and processes employed by Renaissance architects, sculptors and masons in order to build great palaces like this one. These reliefs were intended to adorn the unfinished eastern façade of the palace.

Finally, the **Archaeological Museum** is housed in a group of rooms off the south-eastern corner of the courtyard. This excellent collection was originally put together in the mid-18th century and has recently been reorganised. The clean, modern layout has sculptural fragments suspended on wall grids, spotlit to bring out the detail and drama of these reliefs. Highlights of the collection include a carving of Eros and Psyche, representing sacred and profane love, Roman tombstones whose inscriptions express sentiments no different to those of our own age ('To Marcia Dionysia, the sweetest wife . . .') and numerous early Christian reliefs, one depicting Christ as a homely shepherd, dressed in the typical peasant garb of the Marches region.

The Duomo and the old city

Leaving the Palazzo Ducale you face the solemn bulk of the **Duomo**, one of the few buildings in Urbino that does not date from the heyday of Duke Federico. His church collapsed in an earthquake in 1789 and the late 18th-century replacement is a heavy-handed classical structure, designed by Giuseppe Valadier, with a façade by Camillo Morigia.

The adjoining **Museo Albani del Duomo** (open 9–12.30, 14.30–19.00 in summer, on application to the custodian in winter) contains works of art from all of the city's churches. Among them is a collection of 14th- and 15th-century illuminated manuscripts, a bronze candelabrum cast by Francesco di Giorgio Martini with reliefs depicting events in the life of Duke Federico, and a noteworthy 16th-century marble statue of the *Dead Christ* by Giovanni Bandini.

If you continue uphill along the Piazza Rinascimento you can make a complete circuit of the Ducal Palace. Between the palace and the university, down the Via F. Salvalai, you descend to the beautiful western façade, the **Facciale dei Torricini** (see p.164). On the opposite side of the road is an interesting and simple structure consisting of a spiral ramp that descends to the Piazzale Mercatale. This was built by Francesco di Giorgio Martini to link the palace with the Duke's stables and now (equipped with an elevator) serves as a short cut between the upper and lower parts of the city. Alongside is the Teatro Sanzio, dating to the mid-19th century, and an elegant colonnade of shops following the line of the palace wall and leading back to the Piazzale della Repubblica.

Here is the rather functional Palazzo Municipale, the town hall, with a mosaic of the *Virgin and Child* on its façade, and the more attractive portico of the 18th-century school, the Collegio Raffaello, inscribed with the name of its founder, Pope Clement XI.

If you take the first turning right off Via G. Mazzini, the Via Barocci, you will find the **Oratorio di San Giovanni Battista**, an insignificant little church from the outside, but containing an outstanding fresco cycle, colourful and animated, on the life of St John the Baptist, painted in 1416 by Jacopo and Lorenzo Salimbeni.

The other main road off the piazza, the Via Raffaello, passes the church of **San Francesco**, remodelled in the 18th century and paved with the tomb slabs of Urbino's leading citizens, and climbs up to the **Casa di Raffaello** (open 9.00–13.00 Oct–April, 9.00–13.00, 15.00–19.00 May–Sept). This is the house in which Raphael (born Raffaello Sanzio) came into the world in 1483. The artist spent little time in Urbino for, once his precocious talent was recognised, he was commissioned to do numerous works in Rome, Florence and Perugia, returning only briefly to Urbino to tie up family affairs after his father's death. Even so, the house is preserved as a monument to Urbino's most famous son, with copies of some of the artists' best-known works hanging on the walls. The principal interest of the museum is really the opportunity that it provides to see inside the house of a modestly wealthy family in 15th-century Urbino.

Further up the steep hill you reach the Piazzale Roma with its monument to Raphael, sculpted by Luigi Belli in 1897. The delightful bronze at the foot of the pedestal depicts *The Renaissance*, personified as a beautiful young girl waking as if from a long sleep. To the left of the Piazzale, the Viale B. Buozzi leads to the **Fortezza dell' Albornoz**, a massive fortress built by Cardinal Albornoz in the 15th century when Urbino was briefly subjected to Papal

The imposing façade of Urbino's Duomo

rule. Standing at the highest point in the city, the restored Fortezza affords fine westerly views.

Practical Information

Tourist information office

Piazza Duca Federico 37.

Where to stay

Bonconte, Via delle Mura 28 (tel. 0722-2463). A small, civilised hotel just within the eastern walls of the city and close to the centre.
Italia, Corso Garibaldi 32 (tel. 0722-2701). Inexpensive and very central.
San Giovanni, Via Barocci 13 (tel. 0722-2827). In a quiet street parallel to the main Via G. Mazzini, a functional but clean and inexpensive hotel in a restored palazzo with a restaurant serving modest but good regional food.

Where to eat

Nuovo Coppiere, Via Porta Maja 20 (tel. 0722-320092). Tucked down a side street beside the cathedral this inexpensive restaurant is one of Urbino's best, specialising in boned stuffed guinea fowl and asparagus dishes in season (closed Weds and Feb).
Vecchio Urbino, Via dei Vasari 3/5 (tel. 0722-4447). Top quality and often imaginative cuisine based on game and fish, but closed all winter (Oct–March, and Tues).

14. SAN MARINO

The route from Urbino

There are no direct roads from Urbino to San Marino; instead you have the choice of numerous winding and scenic by-roads that wander through the sometimes gentle, sometimes dramatic landscape of the region known as the Montefeltro in the northern Marches.

Perhaps the prettiest route is the one that heads west for **Urbánia**, originally named Castle Durante but renamed after Pope Urban VIII in 1636. The Palazzo Ducale, dating to the 13th century, was remodelled in the 15th to serve as the summer residence of the Dukes of Urbino; it now houses a small museum.

The landscape becomes more mountainous as you head northwards from Urbania to Sassocorvaro and on to Macerata Feltria, then west and upwards towards the flat-peaked Mount Carpegna (1415m). Well before you reach this summit, a right turn northwards to San Leo passes through a scenic upland landscape of limestone outcrops, isolated farms and sheep pasture, with fields too small and too steep for modern agricultural machinery and consequently still tilled and cropped by hand. By contrast, you occasionally round a bend or descend into a valley to find the landscape scarred by cement works, where the limestone is quarried and crushed, sometimes eating away whole hillsides.

San Leo

Finally you reach San Leo, the most charming town in the Montefeltro, a tiny place built on a hill above the River Marecchia and dominated by its imposing fortress, perched on a rocky outcrop high above the town centre. The sense of anticipation increases as you approach San Leo, crossing first a causeway over the river and then climbing the narrow road, no more than a steep narrow terrace cut into the rock face, before entering within the walls.

You can park just off the tiny main square and walk east to the undulating patch of cobblestones, overgrown with grass, that separates the town's two fine churches. **Santa Maria Assunta** (currently under restoration) is a delightful Byzantine-influenced church with a triple apse, pilasters and blank arcading and deeply splayed windows. Built of blocks of fine-grained limestone and travertine, the church has scarcely changed in appearance since it was built in the 9th century.

Alongside, and equally beautiful, is the Duomo, built in the 12th century

San Marino sits high above sheer cliffs with views that stretch as far as the coast of former Yugoslavia

of buff-coloured stone in the Romanesque/Lombard style. The dimly lit interior is all of bare stone, with a groin-vaulted barrel roof. Two of the crudely carved capitals feature caryatids, one male and one female, and there are two much finer Corinthian capitals reused from the Roman temple which stood on this site before the church.

Below the raised altar, the crypt has simpler columns and the rock-cut tomb of St Leo, covered by a massive slab. St Leo, the companion of St Marinus (the legendary founder of San Marino), is said to have been martyred in the early 4th century, and various pieces of palaeo-Christian masonry, carved with guilloche, lie around the crypt, perhaps from an earlier sarcophagus. Alongside the church, to the north, is the solid 11th-century campanile, rising from the bare rock and worth the climb for the views to the Adriatic.

Better views still are to be had from the magnificently situated **Forte** (open 9.00–12.00, 14.00–18.00). San Leo was the original home of the Montefeltro family until they were appointed to govern Urbino, and the family name originates from the peak on which the Forte sits: Mons Feretrius, the Mountain of Lightning, so called because a temple to Jupiter (renowned for his thunderbolt-throwing) once stood on the cliff.

In the 15th century, Duke Federico of Urbino commissioned the architect of his palace, Francesco di Giorgio Martini, to build this fortress and the result has been hailed as a perfect Renaissance stronghold by no less an authority than Machiavelli, who particularly admired its impregnable position and powerful construction. The Forte now houses a small museum of armour, furniture and paintings and offers panoramic views over the Marecchia valley and the whole of the Montefeltro region.

Equally dramatic are the views of San Marino as you approach from the west and catch sight of the sheer cliff face on which the ancient capital city of this pocket-sized Republic sits. There are no border controls but you know when you have arrived in this independent state because all the car number plates bear the colourful coat of arms of the Republic and because you suddenly meet a dense sprawl of post-war apartment blocks.

The Republic of San Marino

The Republic, only 23 square miles (60 square km) in extent, has a sizeable population, living in nine administrative districts which form almost one continuous conurbation. The citizens, who now number over 50,000, enjoy a high standard of living under a relatively low tax regime and incomes derived principally from tourism. With the coastal resorts of Pesaro and Rimini just 23km away, San Marino attracts tens of thousands of summer visitors, bored with roasting in the sunshine on the narrow beaches of the Adriatic. It therefore no longer subsists on income from philatelists; in the 1950s and 1960s the Republic's large and colourful postage stamps were keenly collected. The Republic does, though, still produce commemorative stamps and its own currency.

The old town

The real focus of interest is the old town of San Marino, perched on a narrow shelf above the vertiginous cliffs of Mount Titano (748m). According to legend, this city owes its origin to St Marinus, a Dalmatian stonemason who was employed in the construction of the harbour at Rimini in the 4th century. He fled to the heights of Mount Titano after the edicts of Emperor Diocletian that resulted in the persecution of many Christians. He was joined here by several other refugees and it is claimed that the mountain was given to this early Christian community by the owner, Donna Felicissima, herself a convert to the new religion.

The continued independence of the Republic into the modern era is remarkable. Every city in central Italy made claims to independence at some time during the Middle Ages and framed self-governing statutes. Few, though were able to maintain their freedom faced with the might of the Holy Roman Emperor or the Pope.

San Marino itself was the victim of several brutal attacks but cleverly formed strategic alliances with whichever partner was prepared to defend the city's independence; now the Dukes of Urbino, now the Pope. In the end, a combination of sheer doggedness, a well-trained army and a near impregnable position allowed the people of San Marino to maintain their liberty where so many other cities failed. It has to be admitted, too, that army commanders often had more pressing priorities or more ambitious objectives than the subjugation of this tiny city perched on a barren rock. Napoleon, sweeping south, made a passing nod in the direction of San Marino stating, ironically, that the Republic must be preserved as an example of liberty, before going on to conquer and loot far richer cities.

As a result, San Marino was recognised as a sovereign state by the 1815 Congress of Vienna. Officially neutral, it has since given home to numerous refugees, notably during the 1840s, when Garibaldi and his companions were given sanctuary, and again during World War II.

For such acts of humanity San Marino has been dubbed 'a den of liberals'. Today, though, it is a relatively conservative state. The constitution has changed little since the 13th century. Two Captains Regent, elected every 1 April and 1 October and installed with appropriate ceremony, head the executive, which decides foreign and economic policy, and the sixty-member Great Council, which acts as the Republic's parliament.

Depending, as it does, on tourism, San Marino makes the most of its attractions, all of which are well signposted. If you arrive in summer, parking in San Marino itself is impossible. The alternative is to park in the lower town of Borgomaggiore and take the cable car up to the capital. The cable car station stands just above the **Cava dei Balestieri**, the Crossbowmen's Quarry, named after the Civic Guard whose skills with the crossbow helped San Marino maintain its independence. Formed before 1295, the Crossbowmen's Corps still exists and in costume demonstrations of their skills take place in the quarry during the summer.

The quarry is surrounded by attractive **public gardens** used as an outdoor sculpture gallery. The bronzes here are nearly all the work of major contemporary Italian artists, many of whom have also designed coinage for the Republic. They include an animated statue of *Maternity*, by Antonio Berti, an abstract composition, *The Bees*, by Bini, a ballet dancer by Crocetti and a skater by Greco. In the tunnel that runs beneath the Casa di Risparmio (savings bank) to the south of the gardens there is a fine nude by Minguzzi.

The **Palazzo del Governo** stands immediately above these gardens, but there is no direct access from the gardens themselves; instead you have to return to the cable car station and follow the Contrada del Pianello into the Piazza della Libertà.

The Palazzo is a recent building, inaugurated in 1894, built in neo-Gothic style to the design of Francesco Azzuri. This is no mere pastiche of a medieval palazzo, however, but a fine example of craftsmanship in the style which, in Britain, would be associated with the Arts and Crafts movement.

A fine stone staircase leads up to the Great Council Chamber. Here a magnificent fresco by Emilio Retrosi covers the main wall and shows St Marinus appearing in a cloud before the people of the Republic against the background of Mount Titano. Marinus holds an open book in which is written the legendary last sentence of the dying saint; 'Relinquo vos liberos ab utroque homini' (I leave you free from (the rule of) any other man).

In the nearby **Basilica del Santo**, the Saint's Basilica, the skull of Marinus is kept in a reliquary beside the high altar. This church, a 19th-century neo-classical building of little character, stands on the site of San Marino's first church, built in the 5th century. In the church of **San Pietro**, alongside, there are two niches cut in the rock which, according to tradition, were used as beds by St Marinus and his companion, St Leo.

Steep pathways lined with souvenir stalls lead to the three **towers**, linked by a rampart, that form the chief goal of most visitors. The beauty of these ancient towers derives from their position, perched on the highest peaks of Mount Titano and rising from a sea of dense green woodland, but with a precipitous drop to the north where a sheer cliff face plummets some 180m into the valley below. The first tower, the **Guaita**, dates to the 11th century, though it was rebuilt in the 15th and has since been much restored. Until the 1960s it served as the Republic's prison but now houses a display recounting the history of San Marino's fortifications.

The second tower, called the **Cesta** or **Fratta** tower, dates to the early 13th century and is perched on the highest point of Mount Titano, on the outermost point of a wild crag. The tower contains a museum of armour, but the chief attraction is the immense panorama; it is claimed that, on a clear day, you can see as far as the coast of Slovenia (formerly part of Yugoslavia), on the eastern side of the Adriatic. The third tower, the octagonal **Montale**, lies isolated beyond the city walls and was probably built as a lookout post in the 16th century.

San Marino's remaining attraction is the church of **San Francesco** in the lower part of the city, beneath the Cesta tower and alongside the city's main gate, the 14th-century Porta San Francesco. The church has a plain

14th-century façade and the usual dull late 18th-century neo-classical interior, but the cloister now serves as the Republic's main museum and art gallery, with some well-displayed frescoes and paintings, including modern works. Key items in the collection are the anonymous School of the Marches fresco of the *Adoration of the Magi* (15th century), Titian's *St Francis in Ecstasy*, and *The Stigmata of St Francis* by Guercino.

Down in Borgomaggiore, in the Piazza Belzappi close to the cable car station, the **Museo Filatelico et Numismatico** displays all the stamps and coins issued by the Republic since 1877, the date when it first began to produce commemorative issues. Even if you are not a philatelist you will enjoy the beautiful design and craftsmanship of the earliest engraved stamps, by contrast with which the more recent issues seem gimmicky and gaudy. A room in the same museum is devoted to Garibaldi memorabilia and the struggle for the creation of the Italian Republic.

Practical Information

Tourist information office

Palazzo del Turismo, next to the cable car station, the Stazione Funivia, in Contrado Omagnano.

Where to stay

Titano, Contrada del Collegio 21 (tel. 0541-991 006). Right in the heart of the city with outstanding views from many rooms and a terrace restaurant (closed 16 Nov to 14 March).
La Rocca, Salita alla Rocca (tel. 0541-991 166). Below the Rocca Guaita with a swimming pool and fine night-time views of the illuminated castle.

Camping: Via de Serrone 594, Murata (tel. 0541-991 299).

Where to eat

Righi la Taverna, Piazza della Liberta (tel. 0541-991 196). In the heart of the city by the Palazzo del Governo and specialising in regional cuisine (closed 24 Dec to 1 Feb and Weds from Oct to March).
Buca San Francesco, Piazzetta Placito Feretrano 3 (tel. 0541-991 462). Good value simple cooking (closed Nov to Feb).
Trattoria Panoramica, Salita alla Rocca (tel. 0541-992 305). Simple and inexpensive, with a terrace for outdoor dining and good views.

GLOSSARY

ambo pulpit from which the Epistle or Gospel is read
cantorium choir loft
cosmati work decorative marble sculpture inlaid with pieces of coloured
glass
dentil frieze small rectangular blocks under a ceiling or roof cornice
gonfalon a picture intended to be carried/displayed during religious
processions
guilloche ornamental carving in the form of intertwined strands
stela upright stone bearing a monumental inscription
transom a horizontal stone bar used to divide up a window space (as opposed
to the vertical bar, which is called a mullion)
voussoir one of the stones forming part of an arch or vault

USEFUL ADDRESSES

Tourist Offices

Italian State Tourist Office: 1 Princes Street, London W1R 8AY (tel. 071-408 1254).
Umbrian Regional Tourist Office: Via Pievaiola 11, Perugia (tel. 075-756 845).
Marches Regional Tourist Office: Ente Provinciale per il Turismo, Via Mazzolari 4, Pesaro (tel. 0721-31433).

Student travel

Centro Turistico Studentesco e Giovanile CTS), Via del Roschetto 21, Perugia (tel. 075-61695).

Festival dei Due Mondi:
Via del Duomo 7, Spoleto (tel. 0743-28120).

Accommodation

Farm holidays

UMBRIA   Agriturist, Piazza B Michelotti 1, Perugia (tel. 075-30174).

MARCHES   Corso Mazzini 107, Ancona (tel. 071-201 763).

Youth Hostels

Associazione Alberghoi per la Gioventu, Palazzo dea Civilta del Lavoro, Quadrato della Concordia 00144, Rome (tel. 06-593 1702).

Self catering/Holiday villas

Cuendet, Chapter Travel, 102 St John's Wood Terrace, London NW8 6PL (tel 071-586 9451) (the UK agent for Italy's largest holiday home agency).

Camping

Centro Internazionale Prenotazioni Federcampeggio, Casell Postale 23, 50042 Calenzano, Florence (for booking forms to reserve places; also buy the Italian Touring Club's annual Campeggi e Villagi Turistici from travel bookshops for a complete listing of sites and facilities).

Caravan and camper hire

E7 Caravan, Bivio Torigiano, San Martino in Campo, Perugia (tel. 075-609 451).

Leisure activities and special interest holidays

Regional and local tourist offices are the best source of detailed information, but you can also contact the following organisations for specialist information.

Wildlife and conservation

REGIONAL NATURE PARKS (Parco Naturale Regionale)
Ufficio Piano Urbanistico della Regione Umbra, Piazza Giotto 42, Perugia (tel. 075-31341).

WORLD WIDE FUND FOR NATURE (WWF), Via Cotogna 1, Perugia (tel. 075-65816) and Via Marconi 103, Ancona (tel. 071-203634), for wildlife and working holidays with a conservation theme.

Summer courses

ACCADEMIA BELLE ARTE PIETRO VANNUCCI, Piazza San Francesco al Prato 5, Perugia (tel. 075-29106) (painting and sculpture).

ITALIAN CULTURAL INSTITUTE, 39 Belgrave Square, London SW1X 8AA (tel. 071-235 1461) (language, music, art history and restoration).

Fishing

FEDERAZIONE ITALIANA PESCE SPORTIVA, Via Piaggia Colombata 2, Perugia (tel. 075-65072) for information on permits and regulations.

FEDERAZIONE ITALIANA PESCE SPORTIVA, Via XX Settembre 3, Ascoli Piceno, 0736-65295.

Hiking and mountaineering

ITALIAN ALPINE CLUB (information on routes and refuges): Via della Gabbiaia 9, Perugia; Via Pianciani 4, Spoleto; and Via Roma 96, Terni.

Hang gliding

FEDERAZIONE ITALIANA VOLO LIBERO, Sigillo, Gualdo Tadino (tel. 015-530 8703).

Horse riding

FEDERAZIONE ITALIANA SPORTI EQUESTRI, Via Flaminia Nuova 213, Rome (tel. 06-327 8457).

Caving

MONTE CUCCO NATIONAL SPELIOLOGY CENTRE, Costacciaro (tel. 075-917 0236).

Walking holidays

THE ALTERNATIVE TRAVEL GROUP, 69–71 Banbury Road, Oxford OX2 6PE (tel: 0865-310399) specialises in guided walking holidays of the countryside around Assisi and the Valnerina.

FURTHER READING

Michael Adams, *Umbria* (Faber and Faber 1964, reissued by Bellew Publishing 1988): a classic account of the history of Umbria.

Hale, J. R. (ed), *A Concise Encyclopaedia of the Italian Renaissance* (Thames and Hudson 1981).

Vasari, Giorgio, *Lives of the Artists*, trans. George Bull (Penguin 1965, 2 vols).

INDEX